[handwritten: Sandra,]
[handwritten signature]

MW00628427

Shoes for the Spirit
Encouragements

[handwritten: Dec. 25th 2006]

[handwritten: "Sister, Merry Christmas" Santa you, Brandy]

A Guide to Your Spiritual Walk
By
Tamra Nashman, L.M., M.A.

Shoes for the Spirit
Encouragements

A Guide to Your Spiritual Walk
By
Tamra Nashman, L.M., M.A.

SECOND PRINTING

Cover design and chapter art by Schlesinger Advertising.
Cover photo by Jono Fisher Photography.
Initial edit, Janie Plante. Final edit, Cathleen Poulsen.

For Further information regarding lectures and personal appearances:

www.tamranashman.com

PUBLISHED BY:
BRENTWOOD CHRISTIAN PRESS
4000 BEALLWOOD AVENUE
COLUMBUS, GEORGIA 31904

To my husband Jim and our children for your support
and patience. You're the best.

Thanks to Gary and Mary for your love, the wisdom of
your experience, and bounty of wise counsel.

About the Author

Tamra Nashman is an educator with a Masters Degree in Music as well as a BA in Fine Arts and has taught on the undergraduate level at both Fontbonne College and Webster University in St. Louis, Missouri. As a licensed minister, she has seminary religious studies on all the major world religions: Christianity, Judaism, Muslim, Hindu, and Buddhist faiths. On the graduate level, she has taught on such topics as "Creation," "Family Structure," "Self-Acceptance," and "Prayer," to name a few.

She is a sought after professional speaker and a gifted performer with numerous original compositions to her credit. She has traveled extensively throughout Europe and North America as a solo vocalist and pianist.

Tamra has had extensive theater experience in such musicals as *Oklahoma*, *Fiddler on the Roof*, *Showboat*, *Cats*, *Dream Girls* and *Phantom of the Opera*.

She has worked as a model and television spokesperson for such clients as Lincoln Mercury, Cadillac, Canon Copiers, Sprite and Nike, to name a few.

With all of these accomplishments, she still considers her greatest achievement to be that of wife and mother. She is happily married with two beautiful children.

Introduction

Life can be a wild roller coaster ride. One minute we're up, the next, we're down. We grip the handlebars and hold on for all we're worth as the curves hit with such velocity; we can barely catch our breath. And, just when we feel like things are under control, whoosh, here we go again! It's certainly not easy and there are as many valleys as there are mountaintops. It goes without question; all of us would love to find the answers to our struggles. Are the answers really available? I believe there are solutions, if we know where to look.

Shoes for the Spirit is filled with personal issues we all face: anger, jealousy, stress, fear, rejection, death and much more. I have found the best answers for walking through these challenges lie within the pages of a book much discussed, but seldom read. The *Bible* offers solutions to every one of our questions; however, it is often the last place we look. How could a historical document have applicable value in the fast pace of today's lives? We spend a great deal of time asking our friends and family for advice. We read self-help books, listen to talk radio and watch videos, DVDs and television presentations geared to address our needs. All of these arenas hold merit. Each one is valuable in the quest to conquer our demons. I have utilized every conceivable mode to transport my difficulties to a place of victory, but I have never found so complete a source as the *Bible*.

Perhaps we mistakenly view God and the scriptures as the great *intimidator*, standing sternly above us like the old English teacher. Her glasses are on the end of her nose, and her ruler precariously held in one hand. She is just waiting for our first mistake. This concept is far from the truth. The *Bible* is a book filled with encouragement, edification, support, love, guidance and objectivity. Numerous examples of individuals just like you and I, struggling with the same battles we face today, fill the pages of this exceptional read.

Shoes for the Spirit takes a Biblical approach in answering the issues we face. It offers helpful guidance as we walk through various emotional, physical and spiritual adversities. I have attempted to make the scriptures user-friendly to everyone, regardless of race, religion, creed, or education. Thanks to the use of the *Touch Point Bible*, a New Living Translation produced by Tyndale Publications, I believe I have been able to successfully accomplish this goal. The *Touch Point Bible* is the most accessible treatment of scripture I have ever read. Straight- forward in approach, the verses literally jump off the page with clarity.

I believe the reader of *Shoes for the Spirit* will be pleasantly surprised to find there is genuine assistance in scripture for every challenge imaginable. There is no denying, the road of life is a complicated one. I don't begin to claim to have all the answers wrapped up neatly in one little book. However, I do believe help is available. And, *Shoes for the Spirit* is a wonderful tool in the workshop of life.

In conjunction with the verses, you will find experiential accounts drawn from my life and the lives of others, bringing a greater visual clarity and heartfelt understanding for the application of each Biblical reference. Names have been changed to ensure privacy, and stories are sometimes embellished for clarity.

This writing has been a labor of love that I have mentally pursued for years, but only recently have been able to script. I have scribbled in journals and dabbled with dreams of authoring a book, but have only now come to that place in the journey where wisdom has finally found a comfortable seat in my soul.

The words written on these following pages are from the heart. I have shared experiences that have been life-changing for others and me, and hope these poignant stories bring home this simple truth-we are not alone.

I am confident of the depths of God's benevolence toward each of us, for I am a grateful recipient of his love every single day. It is my deepest hope that readers will find some of the answers to life's questions using *Shoes for the Spirit* as a tool.

Contents

Trampling Fear

(1)

"Be strong and courageous, for you will lead my people to possess all the land I swore to give their ancestors. Be strong and very courageous. Obey all the laws Moses gave you. Do not turn away from them and you will be successful in everything you do." Joshua 1:6-7.

The air was bitterly cold, and a biting, stinging rain was cutting his flesh like a knife. The thin athletic jacket he was wearing stuck to his skin much like plastic wrap clinging to a hot casserole. It was a miserable feeling, but he had to continue on forcing his body to do what it didn't want to. The mountain loomed ahead of him, huge and ominous, a frightening prospect demanding his full attention and focus. The other riders were pressing down hard now, wanting to be number one, the sound of their pedaling a whir of continual motion threatening to overtake him. He would not be defeated. He had to win this one, no matter the cost.

Lance Armstrong, world-class cyclist, six times Tour de France winner, and all around amazing athlete has a story worth telling. He grew up as a young child without the guidance and love of a father figure, but was blessed with a mother whose supervision and resilience provided young Lance with the kind of role model most of us would only dream of having. She instilled in little Lance important values and directives for success that set him toward the course of his final destiny. *Make every obstacle an opportunity.* This became his motto and the goal that motivated him in every circumstance.

9

His love for cycling began as a small boy around 8 or 9 years of age, when a local gentleman observed his unbridled energy and gave him a bicycle. It was a perfect match for a young energetic kid with a propensity for excitement. It was clear Lance possessed athletic talent and time would prove his ability.

He set about to win every local competition he entered and succeeded where others failed. He then went on to take national competitions and quickly surpassed his own expectations. Before long, he garnered the attention of athletic sponsors and made his way to Europe to ride in the big leagues. Though he was the youngest cyclist, he made quite an impression on the older and more experienced riders. Arrogant and rebellious, he offended many and made few friends, but his talent was undeniable.

At the peak of success, he had won most all the important races in Europe and was giving thought to the mother of all races, the Tour de France. This is a perilous three-week venture across rolling hills and cloud-capped mountains, deep valleys and treacherous winding roads-a cyclists' greatest fear and his greatest exaltation. This challenge is only for the best of the best and those who win it take the podium with worldwide acknowledgement of their unchallenged position in the cycling arena.

As thoughts of the Tour were being seriously contemplated, he began to notice an uncomfortable swelling and irritating ache in his right testicle. Riders are accustomed to pain. Suffering goes with the territory when you spend long hours hunched over a tiny bike with a seat as narrow as a banana on one end and no wider than a grapefruit on the other. He ignored the warnings his body was giving him, and he continued to ride, and ride, and ride. Only when he began to cough up alarming amounts of blood did he actually feel concerned, worried something might genuinely be wrong. After intense testing, he was diagnosed with testicular cancer that had metastasized to his lungs and brain. This is not a prognosis any athlete wants to hear, least of all one on the precipice of greatness.

His cancer treatments were beyond brutal, sapping him of his remaining health, strength, energy, vitality, and reducing his weight to an alarmingly frail number. His sponsors all but gave up on him, writing him off and leaving him for dead. However, the one thing they didn't consider was his indomitable spirit. *Make every obstacle an opportunity.* He would fight this intruder with the same fearless will that took him up mountains and over gravel roads to victory countless times before.

After brain surgery and many months of chemotherapy so toxic even the nurses were forced to wear special clothing to protect them from the radioactive elements of his cancer cocktails, he finally began to get good reports on his blood work and bone scans. *Unbelievable.* Not even the doctors thought he stood a chance of pulling through this.

As soon as he could walk, he was back on the bike, pushing himself toward a full recovery. And recover he did. I admire Lance Armstrong; cancer survivor, six times Tour de France winner, and a man of courage in the face of fear. Please read his compelling story: *Lance Armstrong, It's Not About the Bike, My Journey Back to Life,* Penguin Putnam, Publisher.

◆◆

Spiritual fearlessness rises up with prizewinning boldness when we are aware of God's hand operating in our lives and cognizant of the talents and abilities he had graciously given us. As we utilize those gifts to their fullest, we are empowered with courage and might. We know from the above passage of scripture, that God has directed us to be filled with valor. *Be strong and very courageous. Do not turn away from my laws and you will be successful in everything you do.* Joshuah 1:6,7 As we are faithful to follow God's directives, keeping his objectives as our constant attendant our valor increases. Fear must take a back seat to a heart filled with certainty.

Courage and strength go hand-in-hand. With each fearless step, our spirits are strengthened to godly resolve. And he equips us to handle the various difficulties life inevitably brings through faith in the power of God working in and through us. We have no need to fear anyone, or anything. *If God is for us, who can be against us?* Romans 8:31. Elemental faith now steps into play. If God is real, and scripture is true, then shouldn't we

11

have confidence in his designations and directives for our spirits? We can literally take God's scriptural promises to our spiritual bank, deposit them, believe them, and step valiantly in light of this revelation.

However, if we are uncertain of God's role in our lives, acting on our own strength and making decisions based on our own intellect and physical prowess, we may still know a measure of success. But why go it alone? We don't have to. God has promised to be our guide on this journey, and no one knows better than he the struggles of human existence.

If we can choose to trust in our God-given abilities, and select his wise words as our consummate counsel, fear must step aside. Courage then takes its place as the rightful inhabitant, and we move forward, successful in our quests.

(2)

"If only you would prepare your heart and lift up your hands to Him in prayer! Get rid of your sins and leave all iniquity behind you. Then your face will brighten in innocence. You will be strong and free of fear. You will forget your misery. It will all be gone like water under the bridge." Job 11:13-16.

"Mom, I've got to talk to you about something." Kelsey said, sheepishly.

"Sure babe, what is it?" her mother asked.

"Do you remember when we were at Uncle Taylor's farm and there was a bottle of margarita mix on the counter? You know the one that was suddenly empty?" Mom was busy making dinner, while the laundry buzzer was permeating the air with its obnoxious sound.

"Margarita mix, what are you talking about?"

"You remember; the bottle in the corner of the kitchen in the cabin. You saw that it was empty and asked who drank it?" Mom's mind was beginning to clear now as she turned to face her teenage daughter.

12

"Oh, yes. Seems I do recall that bottle. Now, what were you trying to tell me?"

"Well, Mom the truth is, Caila and I drank that bottle when you were helping Aunt Susan with the horses. I lied to you when you asked about it, because I was afraid you would be really ticked off at us if you knew the truth." Mom was thinking about the label on the bottle; 30 proof vodka mixed with margarita flavoring. *Whoa baby!*

"You drank the whole bottle? What were you thinking?"

"The bottle was only half full, Mom, and it tasted so good, we just got carried away. We got sick afterwards, and we had to lie down for the rest of the afternoon. When we got up, our heads were splitting! I'm sorry I lied to you Mom. I've thought about that ever since we did it, and I had to tell you the truth 'cause it was really eating at me."

The cabin was rented for the week, and the owners had lots of things there the family didn't bring with them. The Margarita bottle was one of them. Mom studied Kelsey's sorrowful face for a few moments before offering her thoughtful reply.

"I'm really glad you decided to tell me what you did, because I had my suspicions anyway. I'm proud of you for coming clean and letting me know about it. Pretty disgusting experience, wasn't it?"

"Pretty disgusting is right!" Kelsey agreed as she grabbed her mom in a big bear hug and laughed with obvious relief.

Secrets separate us from open and honest communication with the ones we love, and from our Creator. A chasm forms, and the only way to bridge it is to open up the lines of communication and admit our mistakes. Otherwise, we begin to fear. We panic about what others may think if the truth is discovered, and we dread repercussions for our actions. Fear has this uncanny way of creeping in like a lioness on the hunt, enjoying the stalk and relishing the moment of attack. Without release, our anxiety owns us, and we are ruled by our fear.

Living a fear-free existence is not an impossible task. Verse 14 of the opening scripture shows us the way. *"Get rid of your sin, leave your iniquity behind you."* Our loving, heavenly Father wants nothing more than to communicate with his children. Once we are out of step, coming back into sync with him simply requires our request for acquittal. If we ask God to forgive us when we fail, much like Kelsey did with her mom, he will gladly oblige us. He is faithful and fair to forgive. He desires closeness with his creation, and there is nothing more satisfying than reaching toward the heart of God and receiving his exoneration and compassion. There is nothing more liberating than choosing to speak truthfully with those we love. This is the pathway that releases us from the confinements of fear.

Have you ever watched a bird in flight carried weightlessly through the air by gentle currents? Gracefully they glide, unfettered and unburdened by any care, completely free to be exactly what they were created to be. As we relieve our hearts of the hidden burdens that separate us from God and others, we are released from the constraints of fear that prevent our spirits from freeflight. We can take wing, *"pressing our hearts, lifting up our hands to Him in prayer."* Job 11:13. We soar gracefully toward the mark of the high calling God has planned for each one of us.

(3)

"God is our refuge and strength, always ready to help in times of trouble. So we will not fear, even if earthquakes come and the mountains crumble into the sea." Psalms 46:1-2.

Not long ago, a hurricane threatened to rip through Florida, smashing the Keys and coming precariously close to our home. The weather forecasters were busy spewing information on technical facts and figures of wind velocity and torrential rains. Clueless as to what all these facts and figures meant, we were certain of one thing; we were in trouble. We sat *glued* to the television for any hopeful bit of news to comfort our turbulent emotions. With every new bit of information the forecast became bleaker. "Are we going to die, Momma?" my little son asked in fearful innocence.

"Of course not, sweetheart. Don't be afraid. We will all be fine." But, I wasn't completely confident we would be.

The thought of losing our home and all the precious things in it was truly frightening. This was a tangible, undeniable fear; one we were completely unaccustomed to and emotionally unprepared for.

We spent long hours removing pictures from walls, lifting furniture to higher places, wrapping the legs of heavy beds in plastic bags and packing my children's belongings for the northward trek. Each toy was examined thoughtfully; realizing the ones left behind may face a sad demise. Such simple decisions can seem insurmountable when danger is the motivation. We wanted to get as far away from the monstrous storm as possible and still save as much of our home as we could. In its disheveled state, our house looked like it did when we were first moving in; sad and strangely chaotic. We didn't know whether to laugh or cry. I turned to take a last glance as I walked out the front door, and an overwhelming sense of helplessness spread its sickening tentacles over my heart. What would we find upon our return? It was all I could do to shut the door and turn the key in the lock.

"You will be kept in perfect peace when your mind is steadily trusting in God." Isaiah 26:3. How do you keep your mind in perfect peace, when your world is collapsing around you? The one thing that kept us sane through the turmoil was the past experience of God's unfailing ability to *provide* for our needs. His track-record was, so far, unchallenged.

Many people were praying for a miraculous turn of events, and much to my relief and amazement, the hurricane took a sudden and unpredicted westerly spin out to sea, leaving our city intact. We all jumped for joy, dancing in a hysterical circle of relief in the bedroom of the Holiday Inn, while tears spilled down my cheeks. I felt my shoulders relax from the tension holding them erect over the past five days, and we took our first easy breath since the initial storm warning.

The "things" in my world—my house, land, and possessions—are so *temporal*. None of them will be my companions on the final ship out of here. Nothing I own can comfort my heart or rescue me in times of need. I have learned an important truth in all of this; when trust is my guide, fear has to take the back seat.

Next time the hurricane may not pass us by, but God will continue to give us his confident assurance, because *"God is our refuge and strength, always ready to help in times of trouble."* Psalms 46:1.

(4)

"For he orders his angels to protect you wherever you go. They will hold you with their hands to keep you from striking your foot on a stone." Psalms 91:11-12.

It was a blue-sky day, blanketed in the warmth and humidity only July in St. Louis can offer. My parents had a small, four-seater, single-engine plane—a Piper Cherokee. On this lovely day, they decided to take my husband and me for a short spin to the Lake of the Ozarks. This was a beautiful resort area in southern Missouri, just an hour or so away from home.

We were talking and having a pleasant time enjoying the scenery below us—green-leafed trees, luscious crops, numerous lakes and tiny winding roads filled an endless map of blues and greens. Before we knew it, we had arrived at our destination and were coming in for a landing. The airport runway at Osage Beach, Lake of the Ozarks, was a short little devil, notorious for giving pilots a tough time, and today was no different. There were several planes wanting to land at the same time we were, and the pressure was on my dad to land the plane. By the time we touched down, we had only a third of the runway remaining, with no runoff. It was absolutely necessary to do a "go around." In pilot terms, this means you must take the plane back up, circle the runway, and attempt another landing.

As dad made the necessary adjustments to get the plane back up, something didn't sound right. The plane was sluggish. He had the flaps perfectly set and the retractable gear up. Thank God, because as I looked out my window from the back seat, I could

16

see the power lines were directly underneath the plane, precariously close.

I had been my dad's passenger in the Piper numerous times. We had made adventurous journeys to every little town and airport in the three-state area. We were "adventure junkies," and very proud of our title. I can still see his face so filled with excitement and wonder each time he got behind the cockpit of that little plane. "Where are we heading, Dad?" I asked with enthusiasm. "Anywhere the wind will take us, babe," was his predictable reply.

In all our travels, I had never heard the plane sound like this. Immediately, he began flipping buttons, frantically trying to get the plane up high enough for a go around, but it was not to be. Silence permeated the air as no one dared say a word. It seemed we were hung between time and space. An enormous explosion behind us shattered the silence. The entire tail of the plane was ripped off by a telephone pole, which speared us, leaving a gaping hole behind the seat carrying my mother and me. From that moment on, it was the roller coaster ride from hell. Our air speed was still 80 to 90 miles per hour, and we were slamming into trees like they were toothpicks. Pieces of the plane were being torn off before our eyes. The wings, the propeller, and other pieces of metal were flying by the windows like rockets, and I knew we would likely die. I realized people don't live through things like this, and I should be afraid, terribly afraid. Oddly, I had an overwhelming sense of peace and clarity of thought. I was actually composed.

When we finally hit the ground, the only clearing in the dense forest, searing heat, and the tentacles of fire were closing in on us. Miraculously, the door had been ripped off. (No small feat, as any pilot will attest. These doors have a huge metal bolt that secures them tightly in place.) Because the door was gone, we could get away from the blaze that now burned dangerously close.

"Get out of the plane. Hurry, run!" My father shouted as he and my husband Jim ran from the plane assuming my mother and I would follow. My mom, however, had been unconscious since the telephone pole speared us. There was no way I was physically able to help her get out. When Dad and Jim saw we were not coming, Jim returned, unhooked my seat belt, pulled me across my unconscious mother, carried me to a safe distance from the inferno and set me on the grass. I had feeling in my legs, but couldn't walk upright, nor was I able to assist anyone else. I was horrified to see my dad standing in the fire, the flames devouring his shoes and pants, desperately trying to lift my mother out of her seat. He had broken his left shoulder and all the ribs on his left side upon impact. Because he was in shock, my father was unaware of his injuries. He began to shout for Jim to come and help my mother. I saw the fear in Jim's eyes as he hesitantly responded to this surreal catastrophe. *Could this really be happening?*

Courageously, he ran back to my parents and tried to lift my mother from the plane. As he took her arms to pull her up, he realized she already had third degree burns on a good portion of her body, as her skin literally lifted from her arms to his hands. He would have to attempt another way of retrieving her from the plane.

Jim reached underneath her hips and lifted her up, carrying her away from the plane as swiftly as possible. We all innately knew the plane would explode at any second, killing anyone still near it, so there was an indescribable feeling of desperation connecting each of us with its invisible cord. *Hurry, please hurry.* The very moment Jim cleared my mother, and dad had crawled to a reasonably safe distance, the plane exploded sounding like a B52 bomber had just dropped a missile in the middle of the Missouri woodlands. The remainder of the plane disintegrated into a million tiny pieces.

I watched all these events with detached wonder. It was almost as though I was at the movie theater; observing some horrific tale other people were acting out. This could not possibly be happening to my family.

Even in my mother's unconscious state, physically unresponsive, she was praying out loud. She was talking to God and praising him for his great power and might. It was amazing to me. When I called her name she didn't answer, but there she was, praying peacefully and praising her Creator. The spirit never sleeps.

Within minutes, fire trucks, ambulances and dozens of wonderful people were there to help us. One of the doctors at a neighboring hospital had seen our plane going down and quickly radioed for help. When the fire chief saw Jim walking around, he assumed he was merely a spectator. "What are you doing? Get back from there, get with the crowd young man!"

"That's my family. I was in that plane," Jim explained. The fire chief's face turned from anger to complete shock, not expecting to see *anyone* alive in such a horrible crash. But, not only one survived, we *all* did.

We were taken to a local hospital and treated for our injuries. My back was traumatized from the tremendous impact, and the muscles locked, preventing me from walking. By the next day, I was physically intact—sore and bruised, but able to get around. Jim, though standing in the fire in long pants and a short-sleeved shirt, didn't have a single hair singed on his head, legs or arms. Even the stench of smoke was absent from his clothing. My parents didn't escape quite so unscathed. They were taken by helicopter to St. John's Mercy Medical Center in St. Louis to the burn unit for extensive skin grafts, careful observation, and treatment.

The next day, Jim and I walked out to the site of our near demise. Nothing but charred ground, trees, and bits of metal remained. The hull of the plane was burned out, with four seats that resembled chicken wire mangled together in a heap. Looking up, I saw pieces of the wings and propeller hanging in the trees, scattered about like some ambiguous puzzle with no border and no meaning. The telephone pole we had speared had separated a third of the way down and swung back perfectly perpendicular. Vines draped the broken pole in an exacting copy of a holy cross you might see at Easter time.

USA Today flew out to see the site and to interview us. Even seasoned reporters, who have seen some incredible things, were amazed we survived such a crash. They commented on the "Easter sign" left for the entire world to see. That amazing pole, in the shape of a cross became the banner of our survival.

The FAA interviewed Jim and my father, stating that in five hundred crashes; this was the worst they had seen. They said people don't survive an event like this—not a single person. It utterly defies logic.

You see God was with us that day. I believe he sent a legion of angels to protect us from death's descent. *"For he orders his angels to protect you wherever you go. They will hold you with their hands to keep you from striking your foot on a stone."* Psalm 91:11-12. God spread his arms around us and brought us safely through our ordeal. Others may say we were just lucky. That's all right. I was there, and believe me, luck had nothing to do with our survival, nothing at all.

In case you're wondering, my mom and dad lived through their burns, subsequent skin graphs, and unthinkable pain and recovered from their injuries incurred in the crash. To look at them, you would never know anything had happened. They are both 85 years young now, and still kicking.

Fear could have overcome us that day in July, but God was right there in the middle of our frightening experience, ready and willing to rescue us. Isn't God amazing?

(5)

"For God has not given us a spirit of fear and timidity, but of power, love and self-discipline." Timothy 1:7.

Every gift given to us by our heavenly Father is designed for our good and his glory. Apprehension on the other hand, paralyzes and steals our joy, peace, and confidence. Anxiety robs us of our pursuits, mocks our attempts and laughs at our failures. As most of us know, fear is a common battle most everyone will fight from time to time and can arise from our own physical perception, human frailties and insecurities. Fear can also be authored by spiritual forces in opposition to the heart and will of God. There is a constant battle raging in spiritual realms to throw us off guard and derail our faith. Whether through the trickery of spiritual foes, or our own decision to allow intimidation to conquer us, apprehension has the ability to bring death to our hopes and dreams. It might be wise to plan a battle strategy to aid us in a victorious outcome against this formidable adversary known as *fear.*

Let's examine the possibility for victory when our fright is brought on by unseen spiritual forces waging war on our hopes. Spiritual battles are the conflict between good and evil, light and darkness. Is it possible to win this fight? Of course, if we put on the necessary armor. No soldier goes into combat without the proper attire and weaponry. Here is an allegory depicting the spiritual warfare we may face and what is required to have the victory.

The soldier stood as still as he could while the armor bearer cloaked him head to toe in heavy protective gear. Outside the tent, battle noises were raging and the screams of dying men were carried through the air like an unwanted messenger. The smell was dirty, filled with grime, sweat, and the undeniable stench of fear. Deftly, the armor-bearer wrapped a wide, sturdy belt around the soldier's waist to give his body the support it needed to bear the heavy arms.

A head popped through the tent door with a look of desperation on its tired face, "Hurry up David, we are in need of help out here, it's getting pretty ugly." The armor-bearer quickly stooped down to the feet of the soldier and carefully lifted each foot into a hand-made shoe, one especially designed for men in battle. He then placed a helmet, formed specifically for the warrior, confidently, but protectively, on his head. He handed him the heavy shield, the one bearing the code of honor, and with a look of resolution, lifted the shiny but well-worn sword from its sheath. The soldier and armor bearer exchanged knowing looks as they parted. What would this battle bring?

The spiritual and physical realms are but a breath apart. If we can imagine separating a curtain and stepping into another room, or crossing a quiet street, it's as uncomplicated as that. Physical armor depicted in the story above isn't so different from what we require to successfully win spiritual battles. The "armor of God" is best described in the book of Ephesians found in the New Testament of the *Bible*: *"Be strong with the Lord's mighty power. For we are not fighting against people made of flesh and blood, but against the evil rulers and authorities of the unseen world, against those mighty powers of darkness who rule this world. Use every piece of God's armor to resist the enemy in the time of evil so that after the battle you will still be standing firm. Put on the sturdy belt of Truth and the body armor of God's Righteousness (right-relationship with God). For shoes, put on the peace that comes from the good news of Christ's love. In every battle you will need faith as your shield to stop the fiery arrows aimed at you. Put on salvation as your helmet. Take up the sword of the spirit, which is the word of God. Pray at all times and stay alert for your brothers and sisters in the Lord everywhere."* Ephesians 6:12a-18.

God's battle plan gives us the upper hand in difficult situations. Knowing the truth written in the Word of God equips us to stand strong by our faith in his declarations. Having a close relationship to our Creator builds our confidence in his great power to see us through our difficulties. Understanding the gospel of peace brought to us through Jesus, calms our troubled soul. Faith keeps us hanging in when we don't know how we can go on. Salvation assures us of our certain future, and the sword of the Spirit is God's words of promise slicing through the giants that threaten. Prayer is our link to God's heart, a sure and certain line of communication to the greatest force the world has ever known. We are empowered when we understand our position in God through *faith*. We can take up our full spiritual armor and stand firm against any tricks the enemy of God may throw our way.

In order to have the victory over fear when we are simply struggling with poor choices and insecurities common to mortals, it helps to know the scriptural benefits at our disposal.

According to the opening scripture in this segment, Timothy 1:7, *"God has not given us a spirit of fear and timidity, but of power, love and self-discipline."* God's *power* is an endowment that strengthens us in the middle of the situation and holds us up when we can't stand on our own. Think of the person who can supernaturally lift a car off a fallen child when this would normally be an impossible feat; or perhaps the individual who can stand and speak before thousands when normally he or she is a quiet, retiring individual. God's power is beyond human comprehension. It is the force that propels us when our own strength is not nearly enough. He has given us the fortitude to use our gifts and talents to benefit ourselves, those around us, and to bring glory to our Father in Heaven. If we can grasp hold of this truth, we are unstoppable.

He has bestowed on us the spirit of *love*, which conquers, mends, and brings healing and forgiveness to all, making us far more accepting of the negligence of others and ourselves. God's love is the benefaction that flows through us in moments of sorrow and pain, enabling us to love far more than we thought we were capable. In failure and in victory, we stand in the knowledge that God has given us *his* love, which endures through every conflict.

Lastly, the spirit of *self-discipline*-other translations refer to this as a sound mind-is a priceless, treasured gift. Positive, rather than negative thinking is invaluable to our over-all peace of mind and freedom from fear. Battles have been won and lost simply through the mindset of the commanding general. Decisive thoughts are imperative in the heat of the fray. Can we allow our hope to be stolen by a poor attitude resulting in a lack of faith?

In those times when we feel overwhelmed by alarm and doubt; we can remind ourselves we are never alone. Whether assaults by unseen forces, or our own human frailty, God has made provision for us through the promises recorded in his word. Through the power of prayer, the knowledge of God's guarantee, a willful decision to love coupled with a positive mental attitude; we can be victorious over the oppression of fear.

Give fear the boot!

Course to a Clear Conscience

chapter two

(1)

"In the end, people appreciate frankness, more than flattery."
Proverbs 28:23.

In committing ourselves to truthful expression, we can genuinely get a handle on walking through life with a clear conscience. Examining our motivations, it's curious what really comes to the surface. Rather than focusing on building up the listener, most of what we say and do is for the purpose of improving our lives, our current situations, or to medicate our own conscience, rather than for the actual edification of the listener. There are risks in being candid with people. We may end up with few friends, and we may certainly make some enemies. Yet, it is needful to be straightforward regarding situations that trouble our hearts. When we aren't willing to be truthful, we suffer the consequences and cause ourselves significant trauma. Below is an example of the need for truthful expression.

◆◆

Jack grabbed the contract from his desk and made a mad dash for the fax machine. Just as he rounded the corner, he caught a glimpse of Ted making his way to Jack's office. Ted had that predictable look on his face, one of defeat and disdain. *Here we go again.*

Falling into Jack's stride, Ted began his usual discourse. "I feel like such a loser, Jack. They expect me to have all the answers, and really, I have no idea how to handle this merger. I

25

never seem to make the right call, anyway. I don't know why they keep me in this job. Then there's Shandra and the kids. We had a huge blow-up this morning before I came to work. I don't blame her if she leaves me. I really don't think she loves me anyway, do you? Nah, what do I have to offer her, other than a paycheck every two weeks?"

Jack rolled his eyes and headed back to his office. *Here's another hour blown.* "Listen man, you can handle this. You've done these mergers in your sleep. It's no big deal. Shandra and the kids aren't going anywhere. What would they do without you?" Jack had spoken these words so many times; his mouth was on autopilot. All the while, he was mentally dissecting the contract that needed to be turned in by the twelve o'clock deadline. A deadline Ted was fully aware of.

Ted was Jack's boss, the one who should be encouraging and leading with strength and boldness. Instead, the employee was the one carrying the employer. This had been going on for three long years, and Jack was growing extremely tired of the emotional burden, not to mention the extra work load Ted's problems were causing. Jack bore the weight of the burden without conveying his inability to carry it, too afraid of Ted's opinion and position to let him know his inane conversations were destroying confidence and impairing Jack's ability to complete his work.

Jack wanted to help him, and perhaps he liked being needed. But, he didn't honestly share his feelings about his inability to cope with Ted's problems, and consequently, he came to a breaking point.

In the middle of a particularly stressful day, with numerous deadlines looming, Ted decided to make his way to Jack's office for another emotional meltdown. Jack immediately recognized the look on Ted's face and before he could speak a word, Jack blurted out, "Ted, you are going to have to take your issues somewhere else. I don't have the time or the patience to deal with this today. Do you want me to do my job, or not? If you do, you must go find yourself another sounding board. I really can't help you with this any longer." Ted's face looked like a wounded boy whose mother had just scolded him. Anger quickly overcame the hurt and Ted turned sharply away from Jack's office door, red-faced and fuming. Jack reasoned to himself, *how can he possibly think I can get anything done with his constant whining? He should know better than to dump his issues in my lap and expect me to have any regard for his position. He's the boss for Pete's sake. He should really get a grip.*

The next time Ted saw Jack at the office, he made an obvious point to head in another direction. The two men didn't speak or have any personal communication after the incident. All office directives were conveyed by e-mail. Jack blamed Ted entirely for the alienation, when in truth, Jack's unwillingness to communicate his needs and feelings was the root of their estrangement. If Jack had only explained to Ted, early on, his inability to carry the emotional load, perhaps the relationship could have taken a more positive spin.

After months of the two men keeping an obvious distance, Jack began to carefully weigh his part in the dissension, and it became necessary for him to confront his fears and willfully discuss the conflict with his boss.

"Ted, have you got a moment?" Jack asked sheepishly.

"Well, I have a meeting in five minutes, can you make it quick?"

"I've been giving a lot of thought to the way I handled our situation, and I need to apologize. Truthfully, I was feeling like your shrink, instead of your employee. I just couldn't get the job done and help you deal with all your personal issues as well. I was feeling overwhelmed and frustrated. I handled it badly, I admit. I'd like our working relationship to be separate from a personal one. Maybe we could go hit some balls tomorrow and have a chance to talk about other non-business issues."

"You're not the only one who's been thinking about this. I acted in a very unprofessional way- put a lot of pressure on you that you shouldn't have had to carry. It's really my fault. A game of golf sounds great. How about 9:30 or so? I'll meet you at the course, and Jack, thanks. Thanks for your honesty and your commitment to this firm. I appreciate it."

This was a huge step for Jack toward honestly facing his past, a past that revealed a pattern of allowing others to unload their problems on his shoulders. Then, when he was no longer able to carry the load, he walked away. Looking back, he could see this was an ongoing and continual life-pattern. He discovered through this incident with Ted, how much easier it was to simply be straight-forward from the beginning.

Are we subliminally taught to withhold honest feelings and emotions, so as not to offend? How can we possibly walk through life with a clear conscience if we repress our opinions and feelings in the belief we must always accommodate others? The story below expresses the importance of honest confrontation.

◆◆

Susan and her good friend Beverly got their kids together on a regular basis for playtime, usually twice a week. Susan and Bev had a lot in common, both Midwest girls, they enjoyed cooking and creative venues, so it seemed natural to get together over coffee, while the kids played in the next room.

Susan's child was expected to adhere to firm guidelines of conduct. She had requirements for sharing and for courteous communication, while Beverly's children had no such limitations. When they went to restaurants, or other public places, it wasn't uncommon for Beverly's children to throw temper tantrums, scream, hurl food about, and basically act unbecomingly if things didn't please them. Susan overlooked these incidents out of respect for the friendship, keeping her opinions to herself. Soon, her daughter Kiley, began to emulate the behavior she saw in her friends.

After a particularly difficult session, the need to confront became clear. Susan sat down with Bev and began an open and honest conversation.

"I hate to say these things, but I must tell you how I really feel. I love Natalie and Robert so much, and consider them part of the family. But their behavior is difficult for me to handle. There don't seem to be any guidelines for them to follow. I understand our methods for raising children are different, and I respect your choices, but Natalie and Robert are allowed to do all the things Kiley is not. I'm having a hard time convincing her to behave in a manner I find acceptable, when Natalie and Robert don't have to. I don't know what else to do, but bring it to your attention. Maybe the kids need to take a little break. I hope we can work this out for our children's sake, and for the sake of our friendship."

Unfortunately, Beverly took offense at Susan's words, and their relationship took a minor detour. However, there was good that came out of it. Susan's daughter got back on track. And Susan discovered friendship without honesty has no solid chance for growth and maturity.

When we can stop hiding behind the veils of pretense, and lay to rest our fear of the opinions of others, we can finally get a grasp on the tools necessary for walking the *course to a clear conscience.*

◆ Examine the motivations of the heart in any difficult situation.
◆ Ask yourself, "What is inhibiting me from honest expression?"
◆ Confront yourself, and the person involved, honestly and lovingly.
◆ Speak truthfully what is on your heart in situations where the clarity of the conscience is at stake.

I have discovered my best relationships are also the most *honest* ones. I appreciate candor, even if it is initially painful. And, when I share my heart in a true blue manner with integrity, honesty, and kindness, the response from others is generally appreciative. *"In the end, people appreciate frankness more than flattery."* Proverbs 28:23.

We don't want to hurt people, and most of us want to be accepted. But when we seek approval by avoiding the truth, it becomes self-sabotage. The paths to a clear conscience are lined with integrity and forthright behavior, both in word and in deed.

Cling tightly to your faith in Christ, and always keep your conscience clear. For some people have deliberately violated their consciences; as a result, their faith has been shipwrecked. I Timothy 1:19.

God has delicately put within each of us a *still, small voice* whose purpose is to lead and guide us toward a path of clarity and right standing with God. I have found on more than one occasion the necessity to *listen* when the voice of God whispers to my spirit. His intention is clear and his purpose is defined. He knows absolutely, without apology, what is best for his creation. The past, present, and future are precisely balanced in his capable hands. When we choose to go our own way, in direct violation to that *still, small voice,* there is usually a price to be paid.

Am I suggesting the human conscience is connected to the voice of God? *Absolutely.* We are formed in the image of the One who created us, and his conscience is placed within our being at the moment we are conceived. As we grow into maturity, we come to *know* when we are making the right or wrong choice. Peace is the quiet indication of our honorable determinations. *"His peace will guard your hearts and minds as you live in Christ Jesus."* Philippians 4:7b.

When my children are disobedient, I am placed in the position to decide if correction is necessary. If the infraction is serious enough, I don't hesitate to reward their inappropriate behavior with appropriate penalization. Without fail, they will say, "I *know* I should not have done that, Mom, but I just *wanted* to!" God looks on our hearts, and knows our intentions. Sometimes he lets us off pretty easily, as we are learning to sail the ship of life through the process of investigation. However, when we become accomplished in navigating the waters, and *still* choose to violate the conscience, the price can be steep. Here's a short tale about the importance of listening to that *still, small voice.*

◆◆

The property was beautiful, bursting with potential-a developer's dream. Sam walked the lush ground many times imagining all the wonderful possibilities. Would it be good for condos? How about a hotel? Maybe we could subdivide, and build homes on the site. The variables were tantalizing. His partners nodded in agreement as Sam laid out a mental visual for their pleasure and for their approval. His gut feeling, one he usually listened to, one that had served him well over the years, urged him toward the condo idea. However, the other partners felt this site would be better renovated for hotel usage. Sam could have pushed harder to get the guys to go along with him, but he backed off, choosing instead to silence the voice of his intuition.

The necessary renovations were timely and costly. The whole process took much longer than planned, and the cost overruns nearly devastated the project. Lawsuits evolved, and the hotel was not open for business for nearly seven months after the projected date. No one could foresee the economic struggles to come, and hotels were the first to take the hit when the market took a downward turn, as no one wanted to spend their extra dollars on travel.

Sam was required to dig into his personal financial reserves to keep the hotel afloat, and the money needed to sustain the project nearly bankrupted him.

He stood on the parking lot of the newly opened hotel, and looked around. The parking lot was empty, with the exception of the few employee owned cars. Sam felt angry and disappointed. *Why God? Why did this project have to tank? Why couldn't this have been successful?*

A clear conscience is one of the most valuable of all spiritual commodities. Without it, we voyage through life, distraught and discouraged. *Some people have deliberately violated their consciences; as a result, their faith has been shipwrecked.* First Timothy 1:19. When we embrace alternatives contrary to the leading of the Holy Spirit of God, we get stuck on the sandbar of life. We lose our peace and direction, and we must face the con-

31

sequences of our own deliberate choices. It is well worth the effort to take the time to listen and obey the voice of God. The rewards are immeasurable.

Father, we pray you will guide our decisions toward the direction you know is best. Forgive our past disobedience to your wise whisper. Kindly reward our faithfulness and pardon our transgression. Help us to be faithful attendants of this treasure of life, and chart our course in a direction worthy of the call you have so lovingly placed on our hearts. Help us to walk the paths of a clear conscience.

(3)

"So the Lord sent Nathan the prophet to tell David this story: 'There were two men in a certain town. One was rich, and one was poor. The rich man owned many sheep and cattle. The poor man owned nothing but a little lamb he had worked hard to buy. He raised that little lamb, and it grew up with his children. It ate from the man's own plate and drank from his cup. One day a guest arrived at the home of the rich man. But, instead of killing a lamb from his own flocks for food he took the poor man's lamb and killed it and served it to his guest.' David was furious. 'As surely as the Lord lives,' he vowed, 'any man who would do such a thing deserves to die!' Then Nathan said to David, 'You are that man! The Lord, the God of Israel, says, I anointed you king of Israel and saved you from the power of Saul. I gave you his house and his wives and the kingdoms of Israel and Judah. Why have you done this horrible deed? For you have murdered Uriah and stolen his wife.'" Excerpts from II Samuel 12:1-10.

Sometimes when we set our mind to do something, our desire can overpower our own conscience. We have the ability to reason with our moral sense, until we have convinced our hearts that we are *circumstantially justified* in our choice.

This scriptural example above is a perfect illustration of a man who wanted something badly enough to override the very foundation of his belief system to obtain it. David literally felt he was excused by his position of power to do whatever he wanted.

We've all made decisions based on our own perceived needs, which we felt were validated by our circumstances. *I've suffered long enough. Now it's my turn to do what I want to do for my own good.* Most people, if completely honest, would admit to overriding their conscience in order to have what they want from time to time. In the narrative below, Deborah gives us a great example of the necessity of attending to the conscience.

◆◆

The dinner party was a week away. Deborah pulled each dress from the closet, checking it critically to see if anything she had was appropriate. *Old, ugly, too long, too tight, too low, too-too.* Nothing here will possibly do for such an important social function. Her bills were piling up, and lately the outflow certainly didn't match the inflow, so purchasing a new frock wasn't really an option. What was a girl to do? The only thing a woman can do in such dire circumstances. *Charge it.*

Without allowing her conscience too much influence, she grabbed her purse and headed out the door to the nearest shop. Finding the dress wasn't so tough, anything looked better than what she left behind in the closet. But locating something in a calculated price range was the challenge. A deep crimson glow was beckoning from the corner. Deborah tentatively stepped toward the gown, secretly hoping she'd hate it. Her fingers ran along the silky smooth contours of the bodice, as tiny pearls caressed her fingers. This dress was dangerous. She slipped it from the rack and held her breath. *I'm in trouble here.* Without daring to look at the price, she stepped into the dressing room and slipped it on. A perfect fit, of course. The reflection of the woman staring back at her was absolutely breathtaking, as long as she didn't dwell too much on the worried face.

Should she look? Of course she should look. But if she knew the price, she wouldn't dare buy it. So, without regard for the loud bells and shrieking trumpets of warning, Deborah took the dress to the counter. She whipped out her credit card and practically threw it at the sales clerk. *Don't look at me that way. I know exactly what I'm doing.*

Holding her breath for fear the charge would not be approved; Deborah said a little prayer. *Just let this go through, and I promise I won't do anything like this again.* Cha-ching. The familiar sound of an acceptable purchase rang in her ears. Instead of feeling elation, a certain foreboding dread sent a chill through her small frame.

The dinner party was delightful, and Deborah and the dress stole the show. She forgot all about her extravagant purchase until a month later when the mailman brought the credit card bill to her front door. She never bothered to check the price until now. *Dear Lord.* Six hundred thirty six dollars and forty-nine cents.

It took Deborah a year to pay for that dress. Grocery bills were slashed, lunches cancelled. Her children had to do with the shoes on their feet, because there sure wasn't any extra money for new runners. The weekend excursion to Disneyland was postponed until the following year.

◆◆

When placed in a compromising position or a questionable circumstance, the quiet voice of the Lord tugs and urges us toward the best path, the path of integrity, if we take time to seek his guidance. Truth is discovered in the quiet contemplation of a listening spirit.

God knows our hearts and he knows our ultimate purpose. He wants to see us use the gifts and talents he has placed within us for our own good and the good of others. If we lose our moral compass in a cloud of inferior determinations, God's loving arms are able to reach and teach our hearts. In a *moment*, he can restore the pure principles of an equitable heart. How fortunate we are to have a Creator so merciful and benevolent to his own creation.

David, though pained by his failure, was brought to a glorious place of restoration through the healing word of truth applied to a seared and battered conscience. David was aware, just like

34

Deborah, that the desire of his heart was not the best choice for him. His conscience was shouting warnings, but he didn't listen. And both of them had to deal with the unavoidable consequences of their actions.

I will always be thankful for God's mercy to reveal the true intent of my soul (*mind, will and emotions*) through whatever means he has chosen. Though sometimes it's a painful process, the growth and maturity that we gain are certainly worth the momentary sting of correction. For wisdom and blessing, a conscience directed toward the heart of God is always the right path.

(4)

"Keep your conscience clear. Then if people speak evil against you, they will be ashamed when they see what a good life you live because you belong to Christ. Remember, it is better to suffer for doing good, if that is what God wants, than to suffer for doing wrong!" I Peter 3:16b-17.

When our decisions are pure and upright before our Creator, we have his blessing. Even though others may ridicule us, God's opinion is *far* more important. Sometimes the right thing is not the popular thing, and we take the heat for making decisions we feel God, rather than our peers, would be proud of. Below is an illustration of following the heart rather than the opinions of others.

◆◆

"Lisa, hurry up girl, you're next!" "Sara, those aren't the right shoes or earrings for that outfit. Grab that bag on the floor and see if you can find them!" It was pure bedlam in the dressing room at Neiman Marcus as twenty, lovely ladies were rushing to make their changes for this televised fashion runway extravaganza.

Just as she stepped out on the runway, hair and makeup flawless, her gaze transfixed in perfect model attitude, her skirt came loose and fell to her feet exposing her granny underwear to five hundred shocked and bemused onlookers. So much for glamour.

35

It was the pinnacle of her modeling career; not exactly New York, or L.A., but she was doing pretty well, in spite of runway mishaps. Television commercials, industrial films, print work and fashion shows filled her schedule. She had little time for anything else, and the money was attractive.

A contract was offered from a huge corporation with national exposure-a dream job! They wanted her to be the spokesmodel for their ad campaign, starring in national and local commercials for their product. This type of opportunity was not common in her area, more often found in the bigger advertising markets. There was a lot of money on the table, and they wanted a positive reply. Thoughts of debts paid, and a possible investment portfolio filled her daydreams, not to mention those Manolo Blahnik sandals in the Saks Fifth Avenue window.

However, she felt it was a conflict of interest, and she wasn't sure God would be completely pleased with her product endorsement. So she passed. Her agent thought she was nuts. Her modeling buddies shook their heads in disbelief. Most everyone she knew berated her for the decision. Here's the interesting thing: she was completely peaceful with that call. Looking back, she had absolutely no remorse over her decision.

When we do what is right for us, rather than what is in vogue, we can stand tall in the face of opposition. Even those who laugh at our determinations are usually the ones to congratulate us in the end. *"Keep your conscience clear. Then if people speak evil against you, they will be ashamed when they see what a good life you live because you belong to Christ."* I Peter 3:16.

I am absolutely unshakable in the belief that a clean and contrite heart before God is to be more treasured than the greatest of riches.

Do we suffer for doing the right thing? At times. However, as Paul so eloquently put it in Romans 8:18, *"Yet what we suffer now is nothing compared to the glory he will give us later."* In the end, it is far better to stand in the presence of a merciful God, knowing we listened to the voice of our conscience rather than the voice of men.

Above all else, guard your heart, for it affects everything you do.
Proverbs 4:23.

Taylor is tall and handsome with sandy blonde hair, green eyes and a lopsided smile that could melt ice-cubes. He's Sandra's favorite boy, her *only* boy, and has never been one to stir up much trouble. The attitude has been within reasonable teenage boundaries, and he's usually consistent with the curfew. He's an incredibly bright kid, the kind who never seems to study, but always pulls in the good grades. Taylor loves to read. Since he was a tiny boy, he was fascinated with books and thought the local library was Utopia. He'll read pretty much anything he gets his hands on. Perhaps that's where the problem started.

Over the past few months, Sandra's been noticing odd behavior. His room, usually tolerable, now resembles a direct hit by a category four hurricane. His eating habits are erratic and unpredictable, strange behavior from a child who could hardly wait to get to the dinner table, especially when his all time favorite meal, fried chicken and mashed potatoes were served. His usually quiet demeanor has become belligerent and disagreeable, almost frightening at times. Usual teenage angst, most would say. Sandra felt the problem was deeper than that. Sandra was right.

After weeks of observing his peculiar conduct, and trying desperately to ignore the chaos of his room, Mom felt she had to intervene. After Taylor went off to school for the day, Sandra stepped cautiously into the darkened dungeon. Buried beneath piles of clothes and dirty underwear, she discovered some interesting reading materials. Satanic cult literature and books on witchcraft were lined up in a row, explicitly open to graphic pages of stories on animal sacrifices and other cruelties. Videotapes, carefully hidden beneath the covers of his bed, all dealt with topics of demonic possession and paranormal activity. *Oh boy, I've got a problem here.*

Sandra left everything as it was and waited for Taylor to come home that day. The door slammed with a loud bang and big feet plodded through the living room. Mom stuck her head around the kitchen door. "Taylor, how about coming in here for a minute? I baked some chocolate chip cookies, and I'd love to have someone to share them with." Taylor stopped in his tracks, looked at his room, looked back at mom, weighing the temptations. He turned in her direction and lumbered into the kitchen without so much as a word.

"I found a book at the bookstore today, I thought you might like. It's called *The Late Great Planet Earth*." Sandra was a smart mother. She knew her voracious reader was interested in things unexplained, and Hal Lindsay's book is an excellent tool in unraveling the mysteries of the war between physical and spiritual powers. It clearly defines the future as it is described in the *Bible's* book of *Revelation*. Taylor grunted, picked up the book in one hand and a handful of cookies in the other as he shuffled off to his room.

A few days later, Mom picked up another book for Taylor, called *The Screw Tape Letters*, by C.S. Lewis. This is a fascinating read written from a demonic point of view. Lewis vividly describes the plots and evil plans against mankind fiendishly carried out with covert malevolence. Mom caught a glimpse of the Lindsay book jutting out from a corner of the backpack on Taylor's way to school. *Oh yeah.*

By the end of the second week, Taylor was making his way to the kitchen without an invitation, casually asking questions about the reading materials Mom had purchased. His brilliant mind was fascinated with the ramifications of spiritual battles and the promises of God's victory in the end. Sandra could see Taylor was weighing things out. However, this decision would have to be his. Only he could choose light or darkness, good or evil, right or wrong. All she could do was hope and pray.

Within a little over a month Sandra noticed some tangible changes beginning to take place in Taylor. He was at the dinner table most nights, whether or not fried chicken was being served.

His room scaled back from a category four hurricane to a tropical storm. He actually said *hello* when he came home from school, and the unpleasant reading materials and videos were missing. (She just had to have a look.) Sandra had done her job in raising this boy. She relied on God's wisdom and Taylor's conscience to see him through. Thankfully, it worked.

It's incredibly important to evaluate what we allow to enter the gates of our eyes and ears. *Above all else, guard your heart, for it affects everything you do.* Proverbs 4:23. All that we see, read and hear affects us. If we guard carefully the things we take into our spirits, then our actions are a direct display of the input. If we absorb negative, hateful, vengeful, hurtful transmissions, through whatever medium, our conscience becomes increasingly tolerant of wrongdoing. Simply put: *garbage in, garbage out.*

The conscience is a gift. Like any precious benefaction, it is to be treasured and carefully guarded. If we cherish something, we protect it, and keep it safe from damage. We set it on the highest elevation where elemental things can't wreak havoc. I have honestly had to make life-style changes to protect my conscience. The videos we rent have to meet a certain criteria, or they stay on the shelf of the store. The books I read need to edify the spirit, or they get placed aside. The "kid shows" my children are allowed to watch and the books they read are considered carefully. This may sound prudish to some, but it is merely a safeguard. Why should I allow my heart and the hearts of my children to be burdened and pulled away from a God centered existence, when the decision is clearly my own?

The path to a clear conscience is paved with the good and upright choices we make. I am talking about the gentle urgings God gives us when we listen for his voice and direction. You may ask, *"How can I hear the voice of God, and how do I know God speaks to me?"* Our conscience *is* the voice of God, and in order to hear him, we daily train our spiritual ears to listen to the voice of our conscience, and to faithfully adhere to God's promptings. The more we choose the path of obedience, the easier it is to obey.

Discovering that delicate balance of a fine-tuned conscience is a lifelong pursuit of the human spirit. If we are not in communion with our Creator, our spiritual thermometer malfunctions, and we lose touch with the temperature of our hearts. We can become cold toward the things of God and unmoved by circumstances and situations that wound His heart. The more intimate our relationship is with God, the less tolerant we become of hurtful, mean-spirited actions, and the less we allow ourselves to engage in activities that grieve our loving Father.

Taking time to read God's Word and spending daily time in prayerful meditation helps to guard our hearts toward a better end and can set us on a *course to a clear conscience.*

Just the right shoe!

Stepping Through Stress

chapter three

(1)

"Save me, O God, for the floodwaters are up to my neck. Deeper and deeper I sink into the mire; I can't find a foothold to stand on. I am in deep water, and the floods overwhelm me. I am exhausted from crying for help; my throat is parched and dry. My eyes are swollen with weeping, waiting for my God to help me. But I keep right on praying to you, Lord, hoping this is the time you will show me favor. In your unfailing love, O God, answer my prayer with your sure salvation." Psalms 69: 1-3, and 13.

Stress is a very real and debilitating malady. Doctors now realize the incredible impact stress has on the human body. Headaches, backaches, short tempers, loss of motivation, confusion, and forgetfulness are all symptoms of stress. The long-term ramifications are even more serious. People suffer every day with illnesses brought on by prolonged tension. With so many variables in our lives producing strain, we are often unaware of the tremendous amount of stress we carry.

I have two children-splendid little people I completely adore-who can manage to drive me totally up a tree from time to time with their continual demands. Having spoken with many individuals over the years about their life issues, it seems that the burden of responsibility toward our children is taxing beyond compare. I don't mean to imply that children bring an unbearable weight to the equation of life, quite the contrary. But, I'm sure most would agree that raising a child is a daunting task.

41

From the time a baby lets forth its initial, primal cry, mom and dad set their antennae to the *active* position and the radar never has a reprieve. There's the fear of crashing the first tricycle, then the removal of training wheels from the bicycle, then scooters, roller blades, racing bikes, followed most precariously by the ever-menacing *automobile*. God help us. Really, it's a wonder there are so many survivors of this profession.

I realized I was in for trouble when my daughter climbed aboard her first tricycle, pointed it down a steep incline and gleefully extended her arms and legs without fear, howling with delight, as the bike careened downward at breakneck speed with a frantic woman running desperately behind. I saw my life flash before me and wondered who would perish first, my daughter or me? Thank God for his protection. I am absolutely positive there is a squad of angels-specifically designed, co-coordinated and highly trained-just to protect this spirited, adventurous, and independent child of mine.

Now that she is approaching the teenage years, the toys are much bigger, far more expensive, and unspeakably dangerous. She wants to drive a car. My husband and I wish she were still riding her tricycle. How did we get here so fast?

Each time my daughter is on her way out the door with friends and my heart skips a beat, I am reminded of one of my favorite verses. Jesus said, *"I am leaving you with a gift; peace of mind and heart. And the peace I give isn't like the peace the world gives. So don't be troubled or afraid."* John 14:27.

Our heavenly Father has a firm grasp on our fears, worries, and concerns. He understands when we feel overwhelmed, and the floodwaters of life threaten to pull us under in their swift current. Our greatest source for peace is to engage in close communion with a loving God. When we invite God to enter the picture, making him part of our family, his divine intervention shows us the way of survival. His love becomes the ground on which we stand and his protection, our serenity. He hears the cry of every needy heart. It's safe to say that he genuinely desires to help us find solutions in every pressing situation. *"Save me, O*

42

God, for the floodwaters are up to my neck. In your unfailing love, O God, answer my prayer with your sure salvation." Psalms 69:1,13.

Stress is a negative force that robs us of our strength and peace. It crushes the spirit with its copious weight, blowing away the remaining ashes like feathers in the wind. God is the great problem solver and stress terminator. It is our choice to ask for help to overcome the forces of anxiety. God is ever available to open the door to peace and tranquility if we sincerely petition him for his help. It's amazing what our God is capable of when we reach out in faith, taking hold of his strong hand. I am so grateful for all the times he has intervened in my family to help us relax and enjoy life as the gift it was intended to be.

(2)

"Even my best friend, the one I trusted completely, the one who shared my food, has turned against me." Psalm 41:9.

"Why did you go to my husband's office yesterday?"

"I was trying to find you, remember? We were supposed to meet at 11:30, and you didn't show, so I figured Keith would know where you were."

"And what were you wearing?"

"What are you talking about, *what was I wearing?* Jeans, a tee-shirt and cowboy boots, why?" There was silence on the line as Jennifer's heart began to race at the tight, angry tone in Mary's voice. "Mary, what exactly are you getting at? I hope you are not trying to insinuate something here. Please think carefully about where you're going with this conversation, as it could be quite costly."

The girls had known each other for more than ten years now. They were more like sisters than friends. Jennifer didn't have any sisters, and when she moved away from her home town and the close friends she grew up with, she felt completely lost. She was thrilled when she met Mary in one of the trendy boutiques in their little town and realized they had so many wonderful things in common. From their first exchange, they just seemed to click like long-lost pals. Mary had an easy laugh and was always quick with a joke. Jennifer loved her company. They both enjoyed shopping and going to movies together, comparing notes on the latest books they were reading, and they often did volunteer work together at the children's center. They were so close words were often unnecessary. Just that look in Mary's eye would tell Jennifer everything she needed to know.

If they weren't together doing something meaningful or mundane, they were on the phone laughing about the latest mishaps with their kids. Jennifer was never as close to another woman as she was to Mary. That's what made this event so painful.

"I think you went to Keith's office because you're interested in him. I think you'd like to make a play for my husband."

"What in the name of heaven are you saying? The thought has never crossed my mind to go after Keith. Are you completely crazy?" Jennifer's breath was coming in gasps and her knees felt as though they would give way beneath her.

"Since you lost all that weight, you have been flaunting yourself around like you can have any guy you want. I can see what's going on with you." Jennifer tried to respond, but she couldn't breathe. Her chest was tight and her throat closed with grief. Her words, laced with tears, finally broke the silence permeating the air.

"One day you will wake up and see what you've done. But, when you do, it will be too late to repair the damage. How you could even dream I'd be capable of such a betrayal lets me know our friendship has been a farce and a joke. I'm going now, and I don't want you to call here again. I don't know you anymore."

Days went by with no contact between the women. After a grief filled week for both the girls, Mary called Jennifer. "I talked to Keith and I told him what I did. He said I was completely nuts to think you'd do something like that. Even my daughter is ready to kill me for accusing you that way. I don't know what got into me. Sharon put these ideas in my head. I think she's jealous of our friendship and wanted to see us torn apart. I was incredibly stupid to listen to her. I can't tell you how sorry I am for what happened. I only pray you will be willing to forgive me."

Jennifer listened intently to everything Mary had to say and carefully weighed her response. "I will always love you. Mary. We had ten wonderful years together. I really believe circumstances and situations beyond our control may have been at work here, but you still chose to believe I was capable of this or you would never have accused me. I've thought of nothing else all week. And, I've come to this conclusion. Our friendship, or my perception of the friendship-and the reality of its dynamics-are vastly different. It's not about what I thought it was. It wasn't as true and honest and wonderful as I hoped. You don't really know me. Even after all these years, you don't really *know* me. It's not about forgiveness, because I forgive you. It's about realization. I've come to realize our relationship is not what I believed it was. I wish you well in life, and I hope every good thing comes your way. But, our relationship will not be the same. I can't change that."

The girls stayed in touch on occasion and held superficial, benign conversations about the weather and town events, but sadly, the trust was gone and the close friendship with it.

The severing of intimate companions, such as Jennifer and Mary in the above story, is one of the most stressful things in life. When we put our trust in another person, making him or her part of our world, we expect a certain loyalty. However, people are people, and we fail each other-sometimes deliberately, sometimes unintentionally. Regardless of the intent, ending a friendship is an anxiety-ridden experience.

None of us is guiltless. I know I have unwittingly and carelessly anguished people, and I've had to ask forgiveness more times than I can count. Once hurtful words are spoken, they can never be retrieved. Once the ear has heard these words, the spirit is mortally wounded. Sometimes oppression leaves death in its wake. Sometimes relationships don't survive emotional trauma. However, God has the power to restore broken hearts and author new life out of a mortal wound. Only He can return us to the land of the living.

We're not expected to continually subject ourselves to painful relationships. Occasionally we have to walk away. We are, however, requested to forgive those who hurt us, because forgiveness releases our spirits to continue the journey of life.

Tension-filled experiences can serve to make us stronger if we hand them over to God and proceed with integrity and faith. We should believe in the strength and character of our own hearts and have confidence in a loving God, who knows all, sees all, and is an active participant in *every* situation we face. He has the power to bring *good* out of circumstances that seem hopeless.

I have a favorite passage of scripture that gives me strength when I feel powerless in situations which are beyond my control. *"What can we say about such wonderful things as these? If God is for us, who can ever be against us?"* Romans 8:31.

(3)

"The next day, Moses sat as usual to hear the peoples' complaints against each other. They were lined up in front of him from morning till evening. When Moses' father-in-law saw all that Moses was doing for the people, he said, 'Why are you trying to do all this alone? This is not good! You are going to wear yourself out, and the people, too. This job is too heavy a burden for you to handle all by yourself. Now let me give you a word of advice, and may God be with you. Find some capable honest men, who fear God and hate bribes. These men can serve the people, resolving all the ordinary cases. Anything that is too important or too complicated can be brought to you. But they can take care of the smaller matters themselves. They will help you carry the load, making the task easier for you.'" Excerpts from Exodus 18.

The phone was ringing off the wall as Todd stood to make a mad dash for the bathroom. *I can't believe I don't even have time*

46

to relieve myself. This is ridiculous. He stood looking in the mirror of the men's room, studying his exhausted face. His eyes were bloodshot from staying up late the night before going over some legal documents, and his desk was piled high with other pressing contracts. *Get with it, Todd. You can't fall apart now. No one else can do the job like you can. There's too much at stake.*

He rushed back to his office like a crazed man, barely noticing the secretary ordering lunch. *How could it be time for lunch already? It seems I just got here.*

"Todd, you've got to solve this building permit issue today or we are dead in the water, man. What are you going to do?" Just as Todd started to give Bob a reply, Jay came into the office as mad as a hornet.

"You're not going to believe this. The city council has deferred our deal for another month. What are we going to do now? This deal will tank if we wait another month for approval. You've got to call Mr. Moore and get him to intervene on our behalf, Todd."

At that moment the speakerphone interrupted with Dick screaming, "Get in here right now! The McDuffin deal is exploding, and you're the only one who can talk any sense into that half-wit."

"Todd, your wife is on line one with a question about the kids. What do you want me to tell her?" Everyone stood staring at Todd, waiting for a response. Even Dick came out of his office, his glasses on the end of his nose, a perturbed look on his face. Todd stared into the assorted sea of expressions and felt more helpless than he had ever felt in his life. *All these people are depending on me to have the answers, and I don't.*

Todd stood up and asked everyone to leave. Exasperated conversations over-lapped each other as the men protested their dismissal. *Chunk.* The door closed leaving only Holly on the phone. "Todd, Todd, are you there? Your wife is still holding on line one." *Click.* Todd disconnected the phones and shut down the computer.

He slumped into his seat and sat with his head in his hands for a long needy moment. *I can't keep going at this pace anymore. It's going to kill me if I don't find some way to lighten this load. But no one else gets the job done.* Turning in his seat he noticed the sun shining brightly through the window. He stood and walked slowly to the bay view. Flowers were blooming in gorgeous hues of red and orange. The water below was glistening in the warmth of the noonday sun and people were making their way in and out of the shops below. *I gotta get a life. I'm so tired of all this craziness.*

Opening the door, he was greeted by a silent, perplexed look on his employee's faces. Calling Dick into his office, he shared his heart. "What can I do? I just can't solve every issue and still be expected to run this company effectively. I'm only one person, but I'm handling the workload of ten. I'm afraid I'm gonna fall apart if I continue on this way."

"Todd, I'd like to bring something to your attention, and I hope you will listen to what I have to say. You don't have any confidence in anyone else around here. You think you can handle it all, that you *should* handle it all. You don't believe anyone else will do the job as perfectly as you can. Maybe you're right. Let's face it, you have more experience, and you are great with people. If we could clone you, our problems would be solved. Since that's not an option, it may be time for you to start learning to delegate. If you believe someone here can do the job 80% as well as you can, then give them the chance to prove it. What do you think?"

Todd knew Dick was right. It was definitely time to make a change.

◆◆

When one is a gifted person, like Todd, capable of wearing many hats, the natural tendency is to go right ahead and wear them all at once. The human head is only so large, even if the ego is considerably larger. There isn't room for more than one hat at any given time. The more we take on, the more stretched we become-much like a rubber band. When we finally are extended too far, SNAP. Something's got to give. Often it's our temper, our health and well being, or our most treasured relationships. The human body can only take on so much pressure. We need to discover our limitations and stay within them for maximum operative function. In disciplining our choices, we actually have the ability to accomplish far more of our goals.

When we are people with numerous interests, it is often difficult to say *no* to well-meaning individuals who know we are equipped to complete a given task. However, just because a person has the *ability* to do something, doesn't mean he or she *should* do it. We need to examine the motivation behind our actions. Are we trying to *please* someone, or *impress* him or her with our prowess and expertise? Narcissism has a way of standing greedily in the way of our need to decline opportunity. Many prideful people have paid a heavy price for their self-fulfilling determinations.

When we refuse to delegate, stubbornly accepting more than we can handle; we tax ourselves and others, too. We are sending a clear message that no one else is as capable as we are, and if we don't do the job, it will not be handled properly. This attitude undermines the morale of our co-workers, family and friends, and sets us up for a fall. No one is irreplaceable, and if we aren't careful, we can deplete our lives in the pursuit of perfection. We put our own soul (mind, will and emotions) in a position of alienation from others, ourselves, and most of all, God.

We don't need to prove *anything* to *anyone*. We have the right to say *no* when we need to. We can recruit, train, and delegate others, trusting them to efficiently complete the assigned tasks. By placing confidence in the proficiency of others, we give a much needed boost to their self-esteem, and we release a measure of our tension, simultaneously. Generally, people want to give you their best when they know they are needed and trusted.

God never intended us to carry the load alone. He wants us to apportion our burdens with friends, family, and co-workers. Our star shines all the more brightly when shared with others. The load of stress is dissipated, and we can reclaim our peace. Moses' father-in-law had it right in the scripture beginning this segment when he gave Moses this wise counsel; *"Let me give you a word of advice, and may God be with you. Find some capable honest men, who fear God and hate bribes. They will help you carry the load, making the task easier for you."* Excerpts from Exodus 18.

If you are feeling overwhelmed, overworked, and under appreciated, perhaps it's time to re-evaluate your motives. Ask God to show you the driving force behind your efforts, and a way to share the weight of your responsibilities with others.

(4)

"We can rejoice, too, when we run into problems and trials, for we know that they are good for us-they help us learn to endure. And endurance develops strength of character in us, and character strengthens our confident expectation of salvation. And this expectation will not disappoint us. For we know how dearly God loves us, because he has given us the Holy Spirit to fill our hearts with his love." Romans 5:3-5.

How important is the role of attitude in a stressful situation? It's essential. We can literally have victory or defeat simply by the way we *choose* to look at our circumstance. How many times have we known people who are belligerently negative when confronted with life's obstacles? There is a total absence of joy in their countenance, and the spirit is lifeless. On the other hand, I have met folks who astound me with staggering amounts of optimism when faced with dire opposition. Who has the triumph? In spite of the outcome, the one who walks with faith and confident hope is unquestionably the victor. Below are two examples of attitude, one of apprehension and one of confidence.

◆◆

"I can't believe it. I just don't get it. I guess I may as well move back home. I won't ever find success in this field. It simply eludes me," Jason grumbled. After all, He'd opened five practices in fifteen years and every one of them left him feeling unfulfilled and despairing. Patients came and went, but Jason's negativity interfered with his success. He kept moving back to his hometown of Charlotte, North Carolina, thinking home held the answers to his despondency.

50

"You are an incredibly talented doctor. People *like* you and are quick to trust your diagnosis. What's the problem? Why can't you settle in and make it work?" His father's frustration had been a constant nagging weight since Jason's first move back home.

The initial practice was riddled with debt and was thousands of miles away from his hometown. Jason was overcome with the financial burden he and his wife were forced to carry, due to a failure to negotiate better lease agreements on his medical space. Jason blamed it on the attorney, but there were solutions available. He chose rather to walk away than to work it out.

The next practice was troubled with an unfavorable location. "It's too far to drive. I'm between towns; no one will journey this far to see me." And they didn't. Practice number three took him back to the safety of Charlotte, his home town. For a while Jason seemed tepidly optimistic. At least he was in a familiar locale. However, it wasn't long until the old negative spirit took the preeminent position, and he was right back where he started. "I should never have moved back. There's nothing here for me. I can't possibly make any money. No one really believes I am as good a doctor as I am. I should never have left the last practice."

Sadly, practices four and five served only to reinforce his pessimistic outlook. After numerous moves, he finally ended up right back where he started, at home in Charlotte. His parents were exhausted, both emotionally and financially, and had come to the point where they stopped offering advice. What good did it do anyway? Jason's mind-set was his greatest enemy. He simply didn't *believe* success and happiness were attainable, and consequently they weren't.

◆◆

She met him in the local grocery store as she was rushing to check out. He made a fast path to her aisle, grinning from ear to ear and boldly stated, "I sure do like that red hair!" He began to grab up her groceries and toss them in plastic bags-all the while making conversation and high-spirited jokes. *Who is this fellow, and what on earth does he want?*

51

On the way to the car, he spoke of his thirty-four year career in the teaching field and the subsequent mishaps and funny stories that accompany such long-term employment. By the time the car was loaded, she was completely entranced with this little man with the grey hair and big, black-rimmed glasses. *What a character.*

Weeks became months and months became years, and without fail, Neal was always the one to carry out her groceries. It was understood. No one else was allowed in his territory. The red-head was *his*. Every week it was predictably the same. Sometimes the stories were different, but mostly, she could repeat them detail for detail by now. She never grew tired of his tales-they were coupled with such enthusiasm, as though they had happened only yesterday. That was one of the most endearing things about Neal; his tremendous zest for life and his love for people. His positive spirit could lift the darkest of moods and put a smile on the saddest face. She knew from experience.

On her weekly trek to the grocery store she noticed something odd. Neal was nowhere to be found. She inquired about him with the local clerk.

"I'm sorry to be the one to tell you, but Neal has suffered a stroke, and we don't know if he will be able to come back to work."

She insisted on pushing her grocery cart alone that day. *Who could ever take Neal's place?*

She looked up his address, and paid him a visit. Not surprisingly, he was the one cheering her up, though the opposite had been the intent. Neal assured her he would be back on his feet and would do his best to again reclaim his position at the store. However, he never fully recovered his strength and was later diagnosed with cancer. Even then, she believed, somehow he would pull through. How could anyone with such an optimistic out-look, be defeated?

She paid him visits whenever possible and was always happier after seeing Neal. He never complained during his illness, only marveled at the wonders of life and offered his humorous anecdotes in his difficult situation. *How does he do it?*

The last time she saw him he was alarmingly frail, his color a clear indication of the seriousness of his illness. She brought him one of his favorite vices; a Cuban cigar. He smiled that familiar Neal smile and said, "I sure am looking forward to smoking *this.*" He never got the chance. Just a few days after her visit Neal passed away leaving everyone who knew him struggling to deal with the loss.

At his memorial a constant thread wove its way through the commemorative words of those who loved him. *He was a man who could see the good and the possible in every situation. Everyone who knew him was a better person for the encounter.* Neal's optimism was one of his greatest assets, and the gift that blessed all those who came into contact with him.

◆◆

Believe it or not, this is all a matter of choice. How we choose to view our world is entirely up to us. We create our own destiny by the attitudes we apply to the various situations and difficulties we encounter. Jason chose to look at his world through eyes of doubt and despair, while Neil took the road of hope and promise. The Lord said he would never leave us or forsake us (Hebrews 13:5b). We have at our disposal a strong tower, a fortress, available to strengthen us to a greater resolve.

Sometimes it seems there is an inordinate amount of time when we are forced to deal with uncomfortable, stressful predicaments. Perhaps the character development God is forming within the spirit requires an inordinate amount of time to accomplish. *We can rejoice, too, when we run into problems and trials, for we know that they are good for us-they help us learn to endure. And endurance develops strength of character in us, and character strengthens our confident expectation of salvation.* Romans 5:3,4. True transformation must come from the spiritual heart of man. The spirit is the vehicle of attitudinal enlightenment and the path on which God desires us to travel.

In walking through stress-filled predicaments with confident faith and expectancy, we do ourselves a great favor. We shift the burden from our hearts to the hands of a waiting God who is delighted with our trust and reliance.

"And this expectation will not disappoint us. For we know how dearly God loves us, because he has given us the Holy Spirit to fill our hearts with his love. Romans 5:5. Our loving heavenly Father has our very best interest at heart. God is working in our lives, through every possible means, for development of our character and the strengthening of our spirits. Stress must step aside when our attitude reflects the heart of our Creator.

(5)

"Don't worry about anything; instead, pray about everything. Tell God what you need, and thank him for all he has done. If you do this, you will experience God's peace, which is far more wonderful than the human mind can understand. His peace will guard your hearts and minds as you live in Christ Jesus. And now, dear friends, let me say one more thing as I close this letter. Fix your thoughts on what is true and honorable and right. Think about things that are pure and lovely and admirable. Think about things that are excellent and worthy of praise." Philippians 4:6-8.

When we are in the throes of difficulty, peace is a most elusive commodity. We need it desperately, but cannot seem to grasp and hold on to the serenity we desire. I have found it tremendously trying when I use all my resources to solve a problem only to discover that it is beyond my control. Perhaps the example below will bring some clarity as to God's peaceful provision in our times of stress.

◆◆

My husband and I had eight long years of financial struggles. Everything we tried seemed to backfire, leaving us further and further in debt. We both had several jobs, just trying desperately to meet our monthly bill commitments, but we kept ending up behind the financial eight ball. We cried out to God for his divine

54

intervention, but the heavens seemed to be brass. I remember the utter exasperation on my husband's face as he made a frustrated decree, "I don't know why we bother to pray. Nothing ever changes. God isn't listening to us." I couldn't help but wonder what needed changing-our finances, or our hearts?

We saw our physical and emotional needs as the paramount issue of life, but God sees the inner working of the character of our spirits as the primary focus. I read the above verse countless times and read it to my husband when I could catch his listening ear while walking through that valley. I discovered some reliable truths. When we set our thoughts on the problem, the problem is all we see. If we concentrate on the blessings of life, the beauty of our world, our family, and our friends, our entire focus is shifted from the struggle at hand and replaced by the virtuous influence of *hope*.

We were telling God what we needed, but forgetting to *thank* him for the amazing miracles we unwittingly observed on a daily basis. During that trying time, my children were well, no serious illnesses or injury to deal with. Our house payments were met as well as our car payments. We always had enough food in the house and plenty of clothing. We had wonderful friends and a supportive family. Our finances didn't change or improve during that time, but our priorities began to make an about face. We slowly began to refocus our hearts on the tremendous blessings God had already provided, rather than the financial woes we felt were incapacitating us.

God was developing some enriching attributes in our core spirit through a stressful time of financial tribulation. We were learning how to *trust*. We were also beginning to understand that life is more than the accumulation of material worth. The eternal value of the spirit and the investments we make in the lives of those around us are what count.

"Don't worry about anything; instead pray about everything. Tell God what you need, and thank him for all he has done." Philippians 4:6. How do we determine the difference between needs and wants? By honestly evaluating our physical needs,

minus the excess trappings. It's important to differentiate between *requirements* for life and mere *yearnings*. God genuinely cares about our desires, and he wants to bless us; however, he has *promised* to meet our needs if we ask in faith and trust him.

When we anxiously worry about our lives, we negate God's ability to answer our prayers. In other words, worry is counterproductive to faith. It also stands in the way of the sufficiency because God finds it offensive. The answers come when God has completed the work in our spirits-no sooner, no later. His response is always timely.

Faith is the great stress-buster. Our faith literally blows doubt and anxiety out of the window. That trying financial time brought us to a new level of confidant reliance on God, and I wouldn't change those eight years for anything. My husband and I are still on the journey of learning to release our stress to a God who hears and answers our prayers. What an adventure.

Father, we pray for your help as we learn to lay our concerns at your feet, knowing you care about our every need. Thank you for your countless blessings and all the prayers you have already answered so beautifully. Help us to focus on what you have already given us, not dwelling on our problems. Thank you for the gift of peace you provide as we learn to trust you. Give us the discipline to think good, lovely thoughts during trying times and the self-control to speak blessings instead of curses. Hold our hand on the journey as we are continually stepping through stress.

Shoe fly, don't bother me!

Jumping Past Jealousy

(1)

"Anger is cruel, but who can survive the destructiveness of jealousy?" Proverbs 27:4.

The theatre was slowly dimmed. Red velvet curtains hung in perfect folded rows from thirty-five-foot ceilings, and above her head was a massive chandelier of twinkling crystal. The old seats, a luscious color of Bordeaux were silently inviting her to sit down. Reverently she lowered herself, anticipating the first plaintive note from the orchestra.

As a child, she sang every chance she was offered. She collected all the Barbra Streisand albums her parents were kind enough to buy her. She sang each note Barbra sang with the same inflection and feeling. Barbra was her own private mentor. As an adult, she used her talent at various functions, gatherings and weddings. The dream of the theater beckoned her from quiet corners of a silenced heart. There was a family to think of, a husband to please, and children with endless needs.

The house went dark as the lights from the stage began to glow. A single note, exquisite and haunting, hung in the air like a bird suspended in flight. The singer stepped from the shadows, graceful and elegant with notes and words mingled together in indescribable beauty. All eyes were riveted on the woman whose voice possessed an unearthly and hypnotic quality. Immediately behind her came a man singing in perfectly controlled harmony, two voices inseparable and magical.

There had been auditions, parts tried for with moderate success. There were little recitals and encouraging words from instructors. Local theatre offered some fulfillment. There were always better voices; someone else usually got the coveted part as she struggled with stage fright, and the paralyzing fear kept her from being her best. However, she sang on without fanfare or high regard, simply because she loved to sing.

Act one closed with a flourish as the two lovers embraced, their voices intermingled in lush symmetry. The curtains slowly came together as the house lights began to illuminate the theatre. She sat lost in her dreams and fantasies. *I should be the woman singing on that stage tonight, if only things had been different.*

She sat through the remaining performance, a swelling anger preventing her from enjoying the program she had saved and scrimped to attend. As the final curtain fell and people began to mingle out of the theatre, she remained transfixed in her seat. Warm tears trickled down her cheeks. She was unwilling to leave this place of unfulfilled dreams and childhood fantasies. *Why couldn't I be the one on that stage tonight?*

It is indicative of human nature to look at the other guy and hold him up as a mirror of comparison, magnifying our own inadequacies. The deep desires and longings of our soul carry us to a place of passion. This sincere emotion is capable of exacting a toll on us, producing actions of both virtue and dishonor.

If jealousy for another's gifts and talents spurs us on to work toward the growth and strengthening of our own abilities, then jealousy becomes a positive force. If jealousy makes us angry and contentious, choosing to walk *away* from our own gifts because of feelings of inadequacy; then we have allowed the emotion to defeat us rather than *compel* us.

This passion can be either a destructive or a constructive force. Only we can decide what we will do with this zeal within our hearts. If God has gifted us all in different ways, he expects us to *do* something with those gifts. Shouldn't we realize the unique qualities of our individual talents and not waste time on futile and debilitating comparisons? *Who can survive the destructiveness of jealousy?* Proverbs 27:4 If we can look at our gifts with acceptance and resolve to be the very best we can be; we will have won the battle from the start. We may not always achieve every one of our goals, but the satisfaction that comes from doing our best with the gifts and talents given us brings a decisive measure of maturity to our lives.

(2)

"When they grew up Abel became a shepherd while Cain was a farmer. At harvest time Cain brought to the Lord a gift of his farm produce, while Abel brought several choice lambs from the best of his flock. The Lord accepted Abel's offering but He did not accept Cain's. This made Cain very angry and dejected." Genesis 4:2b-5.

I have been blessed with two lovely children-one daughter, one son. Our daughter had mom and dad all to herself for eight years. The attention was hers alone and she reigned in the spotlight, princess of a small kingdom. Whatever the princess wanted to do, mom and dad were very accommodating. Whatever the princess desired, she usually received, within reason of course.

Along came baby number two; a tiny son was born. Now the princess had to share mom and dad with the little prince and she was *ticked*. With two much older brothers, I had no experience with sibling rivalry and was at a total loss as to her unseemly behavior.

My usually sweet, happy and fairly well-behaved daughter became a short-tempered, miserable little bugger. The obvious was staring me in the face, but I flatly refused to believe *my* child could be the proud owner of such a nasty character flaw. Where on earth could this be coming from? *It must be a trait from her father's side of the family.*

The simple truth: jealousy is an undeniable part of the human fabric, one of the less attractive characteristics of human nature to be sure, but nevertheless a part of our make-up. Even God gets jealous-we'll talk about that later in this chapter.

In observing the raw honesty of my daughter's emotions, I began to understand the root cause: *fear*. She was afraid we would love our son more than we loved her. She was concerned he would steal away some of the affection to which she had become accustomed. In a strange sort of way, it was a bit like a popularity contest. *Who will mom and dad like more today, my brother or me?*

Once we understood the cause of her erratic behavior, we began to assure her of our love, both in actions and in words. Her comfort level adjusted, and she became more confident of her role within the family.

The book of Hebrews chapter 11, verse 4 reads like this: *"It was by faith that Abel brought a more acceptable offering to God than Cain did. God accepted Abel's offering to show that he was a righteous man. And although Abel is long dead, he still speaks to us because of his faith."* God looks on the heart. He sees our motives and knows if our actions are birthed from a heart filled with love, or greed. He is well aware of our intentions toward him, and toward others. God accepted Abel's offering because his heart was pure before God. He brought his sacrifice willingly with joyous, appreciative intentions. On the other hand, Cain's heart was filled with impure motives. His offering was birthed from a competitive nature, with greed at the core, completely deficient in benevolence. Because of his lack of faith, God would not accept his sacrifice. This created an undeniable tension between the two brothers, which unfortunately ended in tragedy. The jealousy in Cain's heart was a force he was unwilling to address. Because he felt his brother Abel stood in the path of his favor and recognition, Cain took matters into his own hands and killed him. (Refer to the story in Genesis, chapter 4.) The simple acts of self-examination and willing communication could have prevented such a dreadful outcome.

God desires us to examine our hearts-submitting our will to his omniscient ability to see every thing hidden and revealed. He wants us to realize who we are and who we can *be* in him. We have been given a place of rest in God's arms of love. We don't need to fear the opinions of man or live with unnecessary comparisons. Our position is made secure by our faith. In knowing we have that security, we have no need to feel threatened by anyone or anything.

As soon as my little girl realized my arms were always open, her heart began to change. Once she felt safe in her relationship with me, jealousy made an abrupt retreat. How can you feel that same reassurance? Close your eyes and imagine yourself climbing up into the lap of a loving God. Put your head on his strong shoulder and your arms around his neck. Take a deep breath and *relax*. Believe me, this is the safest place you will ever be. And here's the best part; you can go there *anytime*.

(3)

"Don't make idols of any kind whether in the shape of birds or animals or fish. You must never worship or bow down to them, for I the Lord your God, am a jealous God who will not share your affection with any other God! But I lavish my love on those who love me and obey my commandments even for a thousand generations." Deuteronomy 5:8,9a,10.

They were seated at the table waiting for dinner, when her husband made his way to the restroom. In his short absence, an attractive gentleman sauntered confidently over to the table with a big grin. "What's a beautiful woman like you doing alone? I would certainly never leave you, if you were my lady." She was completely taken aback by his overt flirtation and couldn't think of a thing to say. *Hadn't he seen her husband here moments before? What was this fellow thinking?* Before she could respond, her husband was back from the restroom, his face pensive and irritated. "Can I help you, sir? This is my wife Susan and I'm Steven Howard. I don't believe I know you." She could tell by the way he extended his hand; her husband was not interested in introductions, merely departures.

Her husband was not easily given over to jealousy, a strong man with an excellent self-image. However, when interlopers lavished a bit too much attention, his hackles were easily raised. "What was that all about? What a loser. Couldn't he see I merely stepped out for a moment? Some guys have no respect." She was bemused by his reaction, and flattered at the same time.

◆◆

Human beings are territorial creatures. When we become close to someone, we tend to view that person in a somewhat possessive manner. Since we are made in God's image, it stands to reason his emotions may be similar to ours. In Old Testament scripture, God repeatedly refers to Israel as his spiritual wife. In New Testament scripture, God refers to believers as his bride. The relationship between God and his people is one of intimacy much like the marriage of husband and wife. God actually feels jealous of our love and affection. He desires closeness with his creation and wants our attention. He longs for our affection, loyalty, and respect, much like a spouse and partner would desire. God wants nothing to draw us away from the endearment of his heart.

God wants us to *appreciate* his creation, but acknowledge and worship the Creator: to *enjoy* the gifts from his hand but not to live for them. Most of us don't worship fish or animals as stated in the opening scripture of this segment. However, there are those of us who worship money and the power it has to bring us a sense of temporary gratification. We occasionally bow down and show reverence at the altar of power, position and wealth. Who blesses us with wealth? Scripture states *all* good gifts come from the Father above.

I am grateful for the beneficial part of the opening scripture. *"I lavish my love on those who love me and obey my commandments even for a thousand generations."* Not only do *we* stand to benefit when we allow God a place of intimacy in our hearts, but also our children, their children, and on and on…, what a promise!

If we choose to make our Heavenly Father a top priority, we have selected the road of blessing and honor. The benevolent heart of our Heavenly Father will have no need to envy our choices, but rather to bless them.

Is there anything in your life standing between you and a closer relationship with God? Is there anything you love more than Him? Ask for clarity and revelation. He is faithful to reveal those things that jealously stand in the way of God's most intimate heart.

(4)

"'Saul has killed his thousands, and David his ten thousands!' This made Saul very angry. 'What's this?' He said. 'They credit David with ten thousands, and me with only thousands. Next they'll be making him their king!' So from that time on Saul kept a jealous eye on David." I Samuel 18:7-9.

Of all the hotels in the city, this was by far the most beautiful. Tall, and white with architecture resembling a roman cathedral, it stood in the middle of the oldest part of town, regal and commanding. After all the applications made at the various places, who would ever believe her first choice was her only choice. "Miss Thomas, we have examined your resume and would like you to begin work this coming weekend." Trying hard not to sound overly zealous she replied, "That would be lovely. And what time should I begin?"

It was almost eerie how well everything went that week. Naturally, there were a few unpleasant coworkers and a certain number of job foibles, but all in all, things went quite well. Compliments were coming her way, and she gladly accepted each one. Weeks became months and before she could take the time to notice, a year had come and gone.

Just as she was beginning to feel genuinely secure in her job, her manager decided it was time for a change. "Carol, I'm interviewing applicants this week to assist you in your department. I've found someone I think would be great, and I'm sure you will like her a lot." *I'm not so sure I'll like her at all.* But, who could help but like Deb? A tiny, shapely, redhead, she was literally bursting with energy and *joie de vivre*. She was bright, funny, beautiful and incredibly talented; just about perfect in every way. So perfect, in fact, Carol began to feel overshadowed. *What if they decide Deb can handle the job alone? Maybe they don't need me now that someone else so skilled and likable has come into the picture.* As Carol's self doubts began to mount, her job performance declined. She started making inane mistakes on important documents, showing up late for meetings, and basically falling apart at the seams.

"Carol, I can't help but notice how uncomfortable you seem to be around me. Is there something I can do to help make this transition easier? *Leave, just leave and everything will be fine.*

Carol looked up into Deb's imploring face and couldn't hold back her anguish any longer. "I like you very much, Deb. Everyone likes you. Maybe that's the problem. I wanted this job more than anything in the world, and couldn't believe it when they offered it to me. Everything has been great, until you came along. Now the important work is going to you, and I'm taking a back seat to your expertise. I know it's just a matter of time before they ask me to leave and give you my job."

"Wait a minute, Carol, I don't want your job. I have never wanted your job. I've seldom met anyone more qualified for a position. You handle yourself incredibly well, and you don't need to apologize to anyone for your capabilities."

Carol looked at Deb incredulously, not believing her ears. "Do you think management agrees with you?"

"I'm sure they do. You have absolutely nothing to worry about. You should waste less time on petty comparisons and give yourself some much deserved credit."

Carol's perception of the situation was her greatest adversary. How a situation is perceived is ninety percent of the equation. If circumstances are viewed as threatening, then they have the power to become so. However, if honest communication, a willingness to express concerns and fears can come into play, coupled with a realization of individual gifts and talents, usually an amiable solution can be found.

Similarly, in the Old Testament *Bible* story opening this segment, King Saul realized David, Captain of his army, was a formidable force. David found favor with the people after repeatedly making his mark on the battlefield. Though Saul unquestionably held the ruling position, he felt his power was being threatened by a younger, more talented man. Which of us have not struggled with these feelings from time to time?

What if King Saul had been willing to share the limelight with David standing beside him as others applauded? Possibly, the people would have supported Saul all the more. Consequently, the relationship between the two men could have flourished instead of disintegrating. Saul chose the lesser god and became a man filled with jealousy and resentment, which eventually led to his demise.

Envy has great potential for destruction. It is clear how damaging this emotion can be. Let's look at some steps that will give us a heads-up in jumping past jealousy.

◆ Evaluate the situation. Ask yourself, "What is my role in this conflict?"

◆ Know your God-given talents and gifts. Acknowledge your worth without unnecessary comparisons.

◆ View the conflict as an opportunity for growth and learning.

◆ Try not to visualize the other person as your enemy.

◆ Be honest with yourself. Access the situation with open eyes, and integrity of heart.

◆ Pray for God's help in resolving the problem.

◆ Begin straightforward communication with the party involved.

Is it possible to escape the entanglement of green-eyed grudging? Absolutely. We can turn this emotion into something positive by looking at our issues through honest eyes. Acknowledging *fear* to be the root cause of jealousy allows us to begin walking a new road toward a healthy and productive existence.

"But when the Holy Spirit controls our lives, He will produce this kind of fruit in us; love, joy, peace, patience, kindness, goodness, faithfulness, gentleness and self-control. If we are living now by the Holy Spirit, let us follow the Holy Spirit's leading in every part of our lives. Let us not become conceited or irritate one another, or be jealous of one another." Galatians 5: 22-23a, 25-26.

He walked up the creaking stairs, across the weathered porch and grasped hold of the rickety door handle. Carefully, he pulled it toward him and stepped through the doorway. Standing there, he glanced around the entryway of the old house. The air was dank with the stench of aged furniture and timeworn paint. Pictures hung on the wall askew, much in need of straightening. He couldn't help but walk over to the mantle and, with a gentle touch, shift the portrait to a more dignified position. As he cautiously moved his hands away, the artwork lunged toward him, having come loose from the wall. Frantically, he grasped the corner with his left hand, as it slipped through the right and caught it just before it crashed to the floor. Looking back at the wall, he could see the evidence of seasons passed by the obvious discoloration in the shades of the paint. Where the picture fell, the wall was chipping and flaking from a lack of light and air. A perfect, yellowed outline framed the spot where once the portrait hung proudly.

◆◆

Before God is allowed to do his renovations on the quiet, hidden corners of our hearts, this brief story could easily be the description of a life filled with painful memories carefully covered over with a multitude of perfectly placed pictures. When others look at us, they see the lovely artwork, not the tattered soul in need of mending.

Our bodies and our souls (the area of our mind, will and emotions) get battered about over the years through the many traumas

66

and tribulations life brings. Each time we are wounded, we want to protect the bruised areas of our heart, applying some type of covering over the wound. No matter how much we try to mask the pain, we are still vulnerable and traumatized. These emotions and behaviors strip our spirits and cause us to view the world through eyes of envy and judgment-discoloring our ability to see God's great plan for us.

Thankfully, God sees right through the pictures we so nimbly hang on the damaged wall of our hearts. He knows our undeniable need for transformation, which can only happen when his light and love change us from the inside out. He is willing to repaint our lives with colors and textures we can't even imagine.

"Love, joy, peace, patience, kindness, goodness, faithfulness, gentleness and self-control," Galatians 5:22&23, are the shades God uses to renovate the heart of the spirit. The crusty, unwanted, unneeded layers of jealousy and other rancid attributes are lovingly stripped away. If we ask for his help, not only does he clean us up, he deliberately chooses to *forget* we were ever tarnished. By faith we become new beings, and by his grace we are forever remodeled into the image of our loving Lord.

Act your age, not your shoe size!

Climbing the Mountain of Courage

chapter five

(1)

"Don't be afraid, for I am with you. Do not be dismayed, for I am your God. I will strengthen you. I will help you. I will uphold you with my victorious right hand." Isaiah 41:10.

Sarah woke that morning with a knot in her stomach. Breakfast wasn't appealing and after only a few bites, she pushed away from the table. "Sarah, honey you need to eat. You will need your strength today."

"Mom, I just can't put anything on my stomach. I'm afraid I'll throw it up."

"You've played in front of people for years, what has you spooked this time?"

"I just have a bad feeling about this one, Mom, and I can't shake it."

Sarah had always been a performer. She was born a performer and had captivated audiences since her first toothless grin. At the age of four, her mother took her to a string quartet concert where the lush notes of Beethoven and Brahms filled the air. Most small children would want to run and play, but Sarah sat motionless, entranced with the music. As they were leaving the concert she looked up at her mother with earnest, imploring eyes and said, "I want to learn to play like that, Momma."

As soon as her mother could afford the instrument, she started Sarah with lessons on the violin. Mr. Thomas, a renowned teacher, heard little Sarah at her first group recital, and immediately recognized her unique talent. She had a genuine *feel* for the music, she wasn't just playing notes. He took her under his wing and helped develop her skills. The repertoire he chose was perfect for both her dexterity and her heart. She learned to love the music as much as the instrument creating it. Whenever Sarah performed, people were touched as though her music had a direct channel from her soul to theirs. She had a gift, rare and precious.

As she grew into adolescence, something changed. Her confidence began to wane. She began to fear the opinions of others, and doubt her abilities. She grew frustrated with her practice sessions. The hours that had always calmed and centered her in the past, now brought her to tears. *What's wrong with me?*

Mrs. Calloway drove Sarah to the competition at the University. The hallway was clamorous with chattering teenagers and dissonant instruments warming up for their performances. Usually Sarah would be smiling and excited, anticipating her moment in the spotlight, but today was different. Mr. Thomas rounded the corner and caught a glimpse of Sarah's troubled countenance. "Sarah, what's bothering you? You look concerned."

"I really don't want to play today, Mr. Thomas. I have a bad feeling about it."

"That's nonsense Sarah; you know this piece inside and out. You could play it in your sleep. You'll be fine. Just take a deep breath before you start and center your mind on the music. Don't think about anything else." Mr. Thomas gently patted Sarah on the back and gave her a reassuring smile, as he took his seat behind the judges.

Sarah waited her turn as other performers completed their pieces. All too soon it was her time in the spotlight. SARAH CALLOWAY, her named boomed over the loud speaker. She felt her knees begin to knock, something she had never experienced before. Her breath was coming in short, quick, jolts, and she felt light headed. *What is happening to me?* Slowly she made her way to center stage. As she looked out at the hall filled with students, parents, teachers and curious listeners, she couldn't move. Her arms were frozen at her side, her violin a foreign object in her hand. The lights were blinding as she tried to make out the face of her mother in the crowd. *Mom, where are you?* She wanted to run, but her feet wouldn't respond to the command in her head. She stood paralyzed in the silence as the judges regarded her with curious faces.

"Ms. Calloway, would you care to begin?" the judge inquired.

Sarah lifted her violin to her chin, and her bow to the string. She couldn't remember a single thing about the piece. She didn't know the name, the composer, or even the first note. It seemed like an eternity before the music came to her. Faltering and with unsteady strokes she began to play. But there was no feeling to the music, absolutely no emotion, simply notes in the air. Halfway through, she forgot where she was and had to start from the beginning once again. This had never happened before, not to Sarah.

Thankfully, the piece finally ended and Sarah turned from the stage without a bow, so grateful the misery was over. When she reached the edge of the platform her violin teacher was waiting for her, utterly bewildered by her performance. "Sarah, what happened up there? You seemed so frightened, completely unlike yourself." Sarah didn't know what wounded her the most-her dismal performance or Mr. Thomas's disappointed face. She couldn't get either one out of her mind.

This was, unfortunately, the first of many dazzling disappointments. Time after time she attempted to recapture the magic and simply could not get past that frightening experience at the university.

Sarah came to the conclusion she was not destined for greatness in the field of performance. It was time to recalculate her options. Perhaps she could teach violin, or change fields altogether. Music wasn't the only career possibility. It was a sad day when Sarah placed her violin in the case, locked it, and put it away for the last time. *I simply can't play anymore. I have to move on.*

Sarah was raised in a faith-filled home. Her first solo was *Amazing Grace,* played before a full house of appreciative worshippers. She knew her gifts were from God, and she struggled

70

with her decision to walk away from her talent. She wondered why God hadn't been there that day at the University, and why He wasn't there in all the disappointing performances that followed.

A scripture kept falling into her path, like a deliberate old friend. Every time she opened her *Bible*, there it would be. She would read some benign article, and curiously, it would make its way to the page. Even conversations would reveal these words; *"God is our refuge and strength, always ready to help in times of trouble. So we will not fear, even if earthquakes come and the mountains crumble into the sea."* Psalms 46:1,2. What was God trying to say?

Sarah certainly felt the earthquake of fear every time she attempted a performance, and saw the mountain of her ability crumble into the sea with each effort. Her confidence was completely shattered, and she was far too overwhelmed with the despair of the whole thing to venture another try. *I've made up my mind.*

For months, even years, Sarah tried to put the whole thing out of her thoughts, but God wouldn't let it go. Someone aware of her decision sent her an unexpected card in the mail. These encouraging words were hand-written on the inside flap. *"For God has not given us a spirit of fear and timidity, but of power, love and self-discipline."* II Timothy 1:7. Sarah sat down on the couch and began to think about her music. Why did she play? Was perfection her goal? Who did she need to impress? If God blessed her with talent, perhaps the music was meant for his heart.

Sarah walked to the closet and took the old violin case from the highest shelf. She gently dusted it off and unlocked the bolt. She couldn't help but smile as she remembered the beautiful notes of her debut as a six year old child. She picked up the bow, and after a quick adjustment of the strings to bring her violin back into tune, the confident strokes of *Amazing Grace* began to fill the air of the little house. Mrs. Calloway froze at the kitchen sink, not believing her ears. It had been five long years since a single note of music sang through those sad rooms.

With the final stanza, Sarah realized her destiny. She was meant to play. Perhaps every performance would not be perfect. She might forget a note or two, but the heart of her Heavenly Father would rejoice, and he would be there in her strength, her weakness, and yes, even in her fear, to remind her of her call. *Don't be afraid, for I am with you. Do not be dismayed, for I am your God. I will strengthen you. I will help you. I will uphold you with my victorious right hand.* Isaiah 41:10. He would give her the courage she needed. She was destined for greatness, and God would be there every step of the way.

(2)

"'I am God,' the voice said, 'the God of your father. Do not be afraid to go down to Egypt, for I will see to it that you become a great nation there. I will go with you down to Egypt, and I will bring your descendants back again.'" Genesis 46:3-4a.

Keith had dreamed of owning his own business for many years and paid his dues willingly as he brokered real estate deals for other people in order to make a living. Each day he drove by the office complexes and high rises and encouraged his heart with these words; *I'm going to do that one day. I'm going to build buildings.* In order to accomplish his goal, money was a prerequisite, but the family had precious little, and barely eked by on what their joint incomes could afford. The possibility of realizing his dream looked dismal at best.

Tenacity is a gift Keith had in abundance, and he would not let go of his hopes-much like a bulldog clamps its powerful jaws around its prey and holds on for dear life. Nothing could shake him from his objective. Not financial issues, not location issues, not doubtful family and friends; *nothing* could deter him from the target.

He carefully and prayerfully set about locking in a plan to do what he felt was best. He researched the country, looking for the greatest opportunity for growth and expansion, visited the area, and promptly called his wife to inform the family of their impending move. Now, she was less than enthusiastic about this venture, and hoped against hope he would merely *get over it.* But, when this tenacious bulldog makes up his mind, there is no shaking him.

He bravely packed his things and moved to a new state where opportunity was knocking. This was an enormous step of faith, and one Keith didn't take lightly. His vision and desire overpowered his fear, and he took the leap when others would have flinched and walked away. He had to leave his family behind, because his wife refused to uproot everyone without being absolutely *certain* this venture was viable. She was not going to sell the house without full knowledge of a suitable home for their children. In other words, it was *sink or swim, baby-you're on your own.*

Keith came home every three weeks or so to visit and reconnect with the family for a few days, and then he was back on the plane to his destiny. His family both admired him and resented him for his decision. His wife was all alone with two children and a house to manage day and night, while he was setting off to acquire his fortune. *What in the world was he thinking?* However, he systematically carried out his deliberation with great patience and fortitude. God miraculously supplied him with a worthy investor of tremendous integrity, and planted him nicely in a little office, no bigger than a walk-in closet.

Keith's wife paid him a visit, and was overwhelmed with the humility of his new digs. How could he possibly enjoy this environment? He wasn't just surviving, he was *thriving.* One look at his face told her everything she needed to know. He was living his dream. He was working toward his goal. He was *happy.* She embraced the moment with clarity and admiration. Here was a guy she could look up to. He didn't let the odds defeat him. He took the bull by the horns and faced his fears head-on with absolute resolve.

After that visit, the wife was willing to put the house on the market, bolstered by the confidence she could see in her husband's countenance. His courage strengthened her and gave her the assurance she needed to uproot her life and the lives of their children in the hope of something better.

◆◆

In the opening scripture used for this section, the person God was talking to was Jacob. Because of Jacob's obedience to the voice of God, to pack up and leave everything he knew, he and his family were saved from the famine which ravaged their land. They flourished in the new land God gave them. God had set that plan in motion years before in order to provide Jacob and his family with exactly what they needed, *when* they needed it. Isn't it curious how similar circumstances can present themselves today?

God's time-line is infinite. He sees past, present, and future on one continuous score. He carefully orchestrates everything together to create a symphony of joyful sound in our lives when we willingly adhere to the passionate prompting of our heart. Sometimes these directives take tremendous courage, as in Keith's case, but the rewards are often great.

Keith's business is successful. The family is happy. God has blessed them, and they lost very little in comparison to what they gained.

If courage is something we lack, we should ask God to bolster us up in our time of need, and help us see past the *moment* to the hope of a greater outcome. We can follow the desires God places in our heart, if we take one step at a time toward our goal. If we confidently hold the hand of our faithful, Heavenly Father, we will learn how much he delights in our steps of courage.

(3)

"But Moses pleaded with the Lord, "O lord, I'm just not a good speaker. I never have been, and I'm not now, even after you have spoken to me. I'm clumsy with words." "Who makes mouths?' the Lord asked him. Who makes people so they can speak or not speak, hear or not hear, see or not see? Is it not I, the Lord? Now go, and do as I have told you. I will help you speak well, and I will tell you what to say." Exodus 4:10-12.

I fondly recall a time when my daughter, Meagan, was enrolled in a wonderful elementary school in St. Louis, Missouri. She had a dynamite third grade teacher, Mrs. Davis, and was clearly flourishing under her tutelage. I couldn't have been happier with her progress, her school, or her instructor. Everything was picture perfect. Until one day, when my boat was vigorously rocked.

"Hey Sweetie, how was your day?" I asked, as my daughter bounced lightly from the bus steps into my waiting arms.

"It was great, Mom! Mrs. Davis brought a little brown and white hamster to class, and it got loose when we tried to pet it. Everyone was screaming as Mrs. Davis got down on her hands and knees to catch it. You should have seen it, Mom. I bet you would have been down there with her, wouldn't you?"

"A hamster? Oh babe, I don't know, they kind of look like rats, don't they?"

"Oh, Mom, you're so silly! You won't believe what Christina said to Robert, today. Robert told a story about Andrew and it was a big lie, so Christina told him that *all liars have their place in the fiery pit.* Her mother told her that. Is that the true, Momma? And you know what else happened? Robert got so upset that the school counselor came into the room and sat Christina down and told her the *Bible* is just a story book, and you can't believe everything it says. Is that so Momma?"

Oh boy, here we go.

"Sweetie, you know that Daddy and I believe the *Bible* is more than a story book. We try to live our lives by the things that are written there. I don't believe the counselor was correct in what she said. I think Christina was just trying to be helpful to Robert when she told him not to lie. Maybe she could have said it in a little nicer way. Don't you think?"

Meg was already mentally playing with her toys as I finished my sincere explanation to her questions. And my mind was spinning as I began to consider the counselor's words to Christina. I asked her mother about the events of the day, and she readily confirmed the counselor's statements.

"What are you going to do?" I asked, more than a little concerned.

"I will probably have to go and sit down with her to discuss this," replied Christina's mother.

Weeks went by with no contact between parent and counselor. Christina's behavior became more erratic and rebellious. She felt if the *Bible* wasn't true, then her mother was a liar. She didn't need to listen to her mom, dad, or the teacher. The once perfectly behaved student of excellence became a parent's worst nightmare. In my concern, I asked if the counselor's statements had yet been addressed and sadly, I learned that nothing had been done.

After several weeks of watching this whole scene play out, I could no longer sit idly by and do nothing. I sympathize with Moses' pain when he attempted to make God understand the inadequacies and fears of human nature, scripted in the opening passage of this segment. *"O Lord, I'm just not a good speaker. I never have been and I'm not now. I'm clumsy with words."* Exodus 4:10. However, God had a definitive plan for Moses. He was the instrument God used to free the children of Israel from captivity in Egypt. If Moses were unwilling to go and speak, perhaps history would tell a different story. Though my directive was surely less serious than Moses', I also wished someone else would step up to bat, someone more eloquent and gifted with these matter. However, I called the principal, and set up an appointment with her to discuss the questionable comments of the school counselor.

This was not a particularly pleasant meeting. The principal simply did not believe her employee could have been so careless. She assumed I misunderstood and basically told me I had no business getting involved in the first place. However, I mustered up the courage of a protective mother and asked her an imperative question. "If the school counselor did not make those questionable statements about the *Bible*, where did Christina get those ideas, and how can her present behavior be explained?" The principal sat pondering my question, clearly not knowing how to answer me. She agreed to bring the advisor in for questioning regarding the supposed statements. I hoped my work was done, and I had simply raised enough of a question to warrant some inquiry. However, this was not the case.

The arranged meeting required *my* attendance, the child's attendance, her mother's attendance, as well as the principal and the advisor. *What have I gotten myself into?* I was beginning to wonder if I had done the right thing. I almost wished I had simply kept my mouth shut. After all, everyone is entitled to his or her opinion, right? People have the God-given ability to say and do what they choose. I felt my courage waning as the day approached for the meeting.

As much as others have the right to speak their mind, I also have that right. Furthermore, I felt my position to believe in the Bible and the legitimacy of *any* parent to teach such principles, was in question. If a school advisor could undermine years of instruction with a single statement, then how could I sit idly by and do nothing?

The meeting began innocuously enough, and I had high hopes of keeping quiet, but it wasn't long until I was forced to interject my feelings as energetically as the advisor defended. Once we were able to explain the sincerity of our faith, and the desire for respect of our beliefs, the tone of the meeting took a change for the better. The school counselor admitted to having made a statement that could have been misconstrued by innocent ears, and vocalized the necessary apology to both parent and child. She then went on to say something I found quite admirable. She looked at Christina with genuine concern and explained, "Sweetheart, your parents have taught you well. They have greater understanding of the *Bible* than I, and you should always respect their teaching. Please forgive me for my careless words."

I left the school that day feeling humbled. Because I had mustered the courage to speak about my concerns, the result had been positive-restored respect from child to parent, increased integrity in the counselor, and an overwhelming sense of purpose completed within my own heart. God honors us when we honor him. He stands with us when we stand for him, and strengthens our resolve with indescribable courage.

(4)

"Then Naomi heard in Moab that the Lord had blessed his people in Judah by giving them good crops again. So Naomi and her daughters-in-law got ready to leave Moab to return to her homeland. With her two daughters-in-law she set out from the place where she had been living, and they took the road that would lead them back to Judah. But on the way, Naomi said to her two daughters-in-law, 'Go back to your mothers' homes instead of coming with me. And may the Lord reward you for your kindness to your husbands and to me. May the Lord bless you with the security of another marriage.' Then she kissed them good-bye and they all broke down and wept. Orpah kissed her mother-in-law goodbye, but Ruth insisted on staying with Naomi. Ruth said, 'Don't ask me to leave you and turn back. I will go wherever you go and live where you live. Your people will be my people and your God will be my God. May the Lord punish me severely if I allow anything but death to separate us!'" Excerpts from Ruth, Chapter One.

My mother-in-law is a delightful person, and most people would feel extraordinarily lucky to have her. But if push came to shove, I don't think I would be leaving my familiar surroundings to hop on a bus with her to some foreign country if my husband passed on. In fact, I'm certain I wouldn't. I would stay precisely where I was and make a life for myself in well-known territory. What compelled Ruth to make such a bold move, to walk away from her comfort zone into a completely unknown land, strange in every way to her culture, religion and lifestyle? Where did she find the courage?

To better understand her resolve, an explanation of the story preceding the above passage of scripture would be helpful.

In the land of Judah, a terrible famine had swept through leaving crops barren and farm animals dead and dying. There had been very little rain, so nothing could survive in the unbearable heat and parched ground. Consequently, employment was difficult, if not impossible to come by and people were at the point of absolute desperation. Naomi, her husband, and two sons left Judah and entered the adjoining land of Moab in hopes of finding food and work for hire. During the course of their search, they had the good fortune to also find wives for their two sons, lovely girls with good hearts and domestic capabilities. Everything was perfect for a while, but as life often deals us some dreadful blows, Naomi lost her husband and both sons in a short period of time. She found herself alone with two grieving daughters-in-law, and no viable means of support. Women without husbands were destitute in those days and couldn't survive long without some much needed income.

As Naomi heard, God was again blessing the land of Judah with abundance, so she decided it was time to pack it up and head for her homeland. There was certainly nothing holding her in Moab after the death of her husband and two sons. She encouraged her daughters-in-law to return to their families because Naomi had nothing to offer them anymore. Both the girls were clearly citizens of Moab by nationality and faith. Orpah headed back to the home of her parents in Moab. However, Ruth refused to leave her mother-in-law.

The root of such courage must indeed lie in the power of love. Ruth's tremendous confidence in Naomi filled her with the fortitude to do the impossible. She no doubt had observed Naomi's life and recognized faith beyond comprehension that sustained and carried Naomi through insurmountable trials. I believe Naomi treated Ruth with great love and kindness, much like she would her own daughter. There was an impenetrable bond between these two women. And, as compelling as their love for each other may have been, God was unquestionably at work in Ruth's life. It was not by accident Ruth was brought into the family of Naomi. An interesting tidbit: the lineage of King David, and eventually, Jesus the Christ, came through Ruth's second marriage to Boaz, a relative of Naomi, whom Ruth married after her move to Judah. She would never have met this man had she not left her homeland to accompany her mother-in-law.

Was her courage predestined? Undeniably. God set the necessary wheels in motion to bring about his plan and purpose in her life. Against all logic and better judgment, she chose to leave all she knew and commit her life and loyalty to Naomi. Ruth made her decision based on love. God compelled her based on his knowledge of future events. She was chosen to be the bearer of important seed in God's plan, and God empowered her to make a challenging move for the fulfillment of his design.

Sometimes courage is a momentary gift-a supernatural surge that enables us to do the impossible. We may not have time to reflect or weigh out the likely ramifications of our actions; we simply act. For example, the person who sees someone in a car accident and rushes to his or her rescue in spite of fear or danger. At other times, we carefully calculate the options and slowly muster the courage to do what our heart tells us is best. There is nothing in the book of Ruth that indicates whether she made her decision compulsively, or with days of deliberation. She obviously knew Naomi was leaving Moab, and there would be decisions to make. Either way, Ruth possessed a purity of heart and strength of valor God loved. He knew she was the necessary piece of the puzzle needed to fulfill his plan and literally *drew* her to Naomi and the land of Judah by his Spirit. She made the courageous decision, but God enabled her to do so.

Often times, courage is a directive from the heart of God *to* his people and *for* his people. When we don't feel we can climb the mountain, God is there to lift us to new heights of valor. Whether a gift in a moment of need, or a deliberation set about over a period of time, courage is within the spirit of all of us. This necessary giant lives quietly at rest within each heart-a special gift from the hand of God, ready to rise to the occasion when needed. Enacting this gift requires faith-faith in oneself and faith in the God who gives freely to all who ask. You never know what the long-term outcome will be when you choose to act on this amazing gift. I'm quite sure Ruth had no idea her courageous decision would impact future events throughout the years of faith-filled humanity.

(5)

"Keep on asking, and you will be given what you ask for. Keep on looking, and you will find. Keep on knocking, and the door will be opened. For everyone who asks, receives. Everyone who seeks finds. And the door is opened to everyone who knocks." Matthew 7:7-8.

The sky was a crisp, clear blue, the mountains an icy white as we drove in silent wonder around the steep curves to the mountain resort. Everything was breathtakingly beautiful and the skiers and snowboarders looked to be having the greatest adventure. My husband and I were excited at the prospect of spending a week in such a lovely place. Perhaps he could hone his once formidable skills and pursue a shot at the black diamonds. As every skier knows, these are the steep and perilous slopes requiring a better than average aptitude. My mate was a tad bit out of shape, and as I glanced at his protruding belly and listened to his labored breathing, I had some serious doubts as to his remaining aptitude. I, on the other hand, would watch comfortably secure with my cup of hot cocoa and the warmth of a roaring fire.

However, after days of being an observer rather than a participant, I began to grow curious about this sport that so captivated its players. Their expertise made the recreation appear so easy and accessible, even an unskilled sportsman with two left feet like me was lulled into an attempt.

With the help of an extraordinarily patient instructor, I began my ascent-and began, and began, and began. Little did I know the overwhelming strength it would take to move those skis up a simple hill. *Slippery little devils, those skis.* Needless to say my backside and I became the closest of friends that first day. I was covered from knee to posterior with bruises so painful I began to wonder whatever provoked people to attempt this sport. To make matters worse, these adorable little five-year-old children keep skiing up to me in concern with tiny voices imploring, *"Are you okay?"*

"I'm **fine**, thank you." I replied firmly, as I sat in the snow with my knees twisted beneath me. There was snow in my pants, gloves, and nose. My toes were frozen and my lips were blue. "Who chose this sport?" I asked bitterly. Ruefully, I had to admit the fault was my own.

By the time my ski lesson broke for lunch, I had all but given up hope I would *ever* witness the thrill of swooshing down those slopes. What had possessed me to do such a thing? Perhaps it was the narcissistic hope I might look good in one of those tight little ski suits. Or, on a more commendable note, perhaps I was suffering from delusions of grandeur -*mother and child on the slopes, having a wonderful time.* Who was I kidding? All these thoughts filled my mind as I slumped with exhaustion into my seat, barely able to bring a spoon full of warm soup to my frozen lips. I declared emphatically to my husband, who surprisingly was handling the double black diamonds with ease, "I will *never* do this again. Why did you talk me into this?" Of course, he didn't talk me into *anything,* but I had to blame someone for my misery.

My charming and notably attractive instructor, Herve, complete with an adorable French accent, encouraged me by saying, *"Come now Tam-a-ra* (in French you see, there is always another syllable to your name), *of course you can do thees. Eets not hard. I weel help you become a reel skier!"* Well, who could resist that? And, back out to the slopes I went.

I looked up at the mountain, and it looked down at me with tremendous pity. I could almost hear it moan, *Oh dear, here she comes again.* On this attempt, Herve decided we needed to take the higher lift, to *really* get a feel for the skis. My first time off the lift I went barreling into a ten-foot snowdrift, and my classmates had to dig me out with their ski poles. As I lay there covered in snow and frozen to the bone, I kept mumbling to myself, *"I wanted to do this; I really wanted to do this."* However, I must admit this time was a *little* easier. I fell only half as often, wretched my knees in manageable ways, ate far less snow, and became a little giddy with the thought that I was getting the hang of it. I was so happy I made it down the slope; I danced to the ski lift. This is an interesting trick with four and a half feet of plywood on your shoes.

Let's talk about those shoes. Here's a girl who loves her Vera Wang's, Stewart Weitzman's, and Nine West's. Who designed these things, anyway? They are huge, cumbersome, heavy, grossly uncomfortable, and esthetically outrageous. Give me my three-inch heels baby, and I'll show ya how to ski down these slopes in vogue.

When the day was finished and I lumbered heroically back to the hotel room, it took every ounce of remaining strength I could muster to pull those ugly boots off my battered feet. One look in the mirror at my naked and badly bruised body was proof of my folly. Forty-five-year-old women should write books.

However, my indomitable spirit prevailed. I would not let that mountain defeat me. No way. So, the next day I dutifully donned my gear, with a little extra padding on the backside, and ventured up the mountain again. I don't know if my classmates were happy to see me, or just feeling sorry for me, but their kindness bolstered my flagging spirit as I looked up at that mountain, wondering what the heck I was doing here *again.*

I attacked the challenge with great courage, renewed fortitude, and a lot of prayer. I knew God made this mountain and he made me, and I'm quite sure he was wondering what on earth I was trying to prove. But he humored me, and probably sent an angel or two to keep me from breaking my neck. And I am happy to report, I actually took the ski lift no less than ten times, skiing down with better than adequate turns, properly negotiating skillful stops, and didn't eat snow one time. *Yes!*

Now you've read this ridiculous, but quite true story, and you're asking yourself, what could this possibly have to do with the scripture in this opening segment? Oh come on, you get it.

Sometimes courage is about not giving up-in spite of the odds, or the challenge, or even human capability. If we want something badly enough to keep *asking, looking, knocking and seeking*, we can have it and we can achieve it.

It took courage for me to attempt that mountain. But I did it. Whatever your mountain is, you can climb it, too. Just enlist a little faith, and see what you can accomplish. You might surprise yourself.

It's not the time to get cold feet!

Dancing Beyond Depression

chapter six

(1)

"Oh Lord, you have examined my heart and know everything about me. You know when I sit down or stand up. You know my every thought when far away. You chart the path ahead of me and tell me where to stop and rest. Such knowledge is too wonderful for me, too great for me to know! I can never get away from your presence! If I go up to heaven you are there; if I go down to the place of the dead, you are there. If I ride the wings of the morning, if I dwell by the farthest oceans, even there you hand will guide me, and your strength will support me. I could ask the darkness to hide me, and the light around me to become night, but even in darkness I cannot hide from you. To you the night shines as bright as day. Darkness and light are both alike to you." Excerpts from Psalms 139.

It was another dark day as Marcy pulled her jeans on and tied her tennis shoes. *I can't go today. I just can't go.*

"Marcy, hurry up or you'll be late again. You know I can't show up past 8:30 or Mr. Connor will have my head. Get a move on!"

"I'm not feeling good today, Mom. I really think I should stay home."

"You've missed so much school this year; they won't let you move up to the next grade. What on earth is going on with you?" Marcy's mom demanded.

Mrs. Stubbin was having a tough time supporting herself and her daughter on a limited income. She had tremendous financial worries since her husband left her the first part of last year. She knew Marcy was having a difficult time with the divorce and the money crunch, but Mom had a lot on her plate and very little excess time or energy to deal with a troubled teenager.

For Marcy, some days were filled with laughter and sunshine as adolescence should be, while far too many others were shrouded in a dark debilitating fear of failure and overwhelming sense of despair. Several of her friends suffered with various forms of teenage anxiety, but Marcy's was far beyond general juvenile angst. There were days she couldn't crawl out of bed and get ready for school. She told her mother she simply wasn't feeling well, but mentioned nothing of her despondency. *It's probably my fault dad left.*

Self-doubt and disgust haunted her relentlessly. She felt inadequate, always falling short of the expectations of her parents, teachers and peers. No matter how much she tried, she couldn't remember all the things she needed to, and it was an impossible task to concentrate in class. Her grades were a representation of her difficulties and an affirmation of her incompetence. She struggled with attention deficit disorder, but no one had a label for her malady in those days.

To look at her from the outside revealed nothing of the tremendous pain she carried. Marcy possessed many wonderful talents and got along well with people. She exhibited tremendous compassion in those times when her friends needed encouragement and always came forward with a humorous anecdote for their trying situations. Her loving nature affirmed and encouraged those around her. But Marcy couldn't see her own worth and value, and wasn't able to help herself.

All too often her weekends were spent locked away in her room, the lights out, curtains closed, and Marcy huddled in the corner with her childhood blanket wrapped securely around her frail body. She cried in silence, her tears hidden from her friends and her mother. She kept them all away on those dark days and concealed her malaise as best she could, but the walls were closing in and the shadows were growing darker.

She awoke one morning with a clear plan in mind to relieve her suffering. She feigned another sick day and waited until she heard the garage door shut as her mother left for work. She cautiously stole to Mom's medicine cabinet. *There has to be something in here that will put me to sleep.* Sure enough, there on the shelf was a prescription sleeping pill, and the bottle was full. *Do not take more than the prescribed dosage or serious injury and possible death could occur.* The warning was clearly marked on the bottle, and Marcy understood the dangers of what she was contemplating. *I can't go on like this anymore. If I can just go to sleep, it will all be over.* She reached for the bottle in the medicine cabinet, her hand shaking. She held it close to her heart for a decisive moment, and then turned from the bathroom. Engrossed in the label, she didn't notice the book at the edge of the dresser as she brushed by on her way to the kitchen. SLAM. The book was big and black and landed on the tile floor with resounding clarity, almost as if it wanted her attention. Startled and in need of a distraction, she bent down to pick up the book. As she flipped it over her eyes fell on these words; *I could ask the darkness to hide me and the light around me to become night, but even in darkness I cannot hide from you. To you the night shines as bright as day.* Surprised and curious, she backed up a paragraph. *I can never get away from your presence! If I go up to heaven you are there; if I go down to the place of the dead, you are there.* Marcy knew this was not an accident. Was God speaking to her?

She sat down on the cold tile and started reading Psalm 139 from the big, black *Bible* that had fallen at her feet. The words on the page became life to her in that moment of contemplated death and the light of warmth and revelation poured into her reticent spirit. She began to understand that she could *choose* darkness. She could *choose* depression, and even then, God would not leave or forsake her. *To you the night shines as bright as day. Darkness and light are both alike to you.*

Was God here in her darkest moment to show her his faithful love? She slowly began to realize the important truth expressed in these illuminating scriptures-life is a matter of *perception*. If God is *there* in our darkness, or in our light, perhaps we could begin to *view* our world through his eyes. If we could see our lives through the eyes of our Creator, then our sense of value would be defined by entirely new criteria. If the God of the universe knows our thoughts, cares about our comings and goings, knows where we are at any given moment, and wants to guide, strengthen and support us, then we *should* look at life through eyes of hope and not despair.

Marcy got up from that cold floor a different girl than the one who sat down moments before. She took the sleeping pills back to the medicine cabinet and placed them on the shelf where she found them. This time her hand wasn't shaking. She knew something wonderful she didn't know before. *She was not now, and would never be, alone. God loves her just as she is.*

(2)

"Then Jesus said, 'Come to me, all of you who are weary and carry heavy burdens, and I will give you rest.'" Matthew 11:28.

As a singer and public speaker, the voice is the key instrument in all I do. Without it I am pretty much like a ship stuck on a sandbar, going absolutely nowhere. The problem had been creeping up on me for months, and I was doing my best to ignore it. After all, the calendar was full of various events requiring me to either talk, or sing. How could I cancel when people were depending on me? But, there was no denying, my voice was becoming increasingly hoarse, as if I'd shouted long and hard at a baseball game. I tried to work around it, actually brushing aside the problem in hopes it would somehow correct itself. Hot tea and honey was my home-made medicine, and I lived on Halls cough drops. However, I finally had to admit, I was not getting any better; in fact, I was getting worse. Off I trotted to the specialist in hopes he would give me a pill or a shot, to bring me some instant improvement. Unfortunately, this was not a McDonald's drive through situation.

"You need at least two weeks of silence and rest. You shouldn't talk and don't even think about singing," the doctor casually diagnosed. *You've got to be kidding me.* I opened my mouth to argue his conclusions and was met with a resounding *shhhh!* I left the office that day wondering what on earth I would do without the ability to speak. I realize that I talk all the time. I talk to my husband, my children, my friends, *myself;* the last person on my list, arguably the most attentive. Perhaps my problem was a blessing for all who were forced to endure my ramblings.

However, try correcting children without speaking. Each time I attempted to discipline them with faltering pantomime, they would giggle and run in the other room. Whenever the phone rang, I would have to resist the urge to grab it, a tug of war raging between my hand and my brain. It's impossible to imagine how much the voice is utilized during the course of each day, until you don't have it. Sign language is a challenging alternative when you're accustomed to expressing yourself with the nuance only the human voice can offer.

Darker thoughts began to crowd my mind. *What if I never sing again? What if I lose my normal speaking voice? What kind of lifestyle changes will I need to make?* A feeling of loss began to overwhelm my heart, and I realized a genuine sense of grief, much like the death of something dear.

After two grueling weeks of silence, I went back to the doctor. *Dear God, let this be good news.* The node on my vocal cord, which was causing the hoarseness, was gone. What a relief. But I couldn't help but wonder if it would come back as soon as I started to sing again. I tried out my cords the following weekend. They sounded better than they had in months, however, the very next day I was hoarse again. I felt myself sinking in a quagmire of despair. I was questioning whether or not this would be an ongoing problem, altering my lifestyle and affecting my work.

Thank God for my daughter, Meagan. She was so loving and caring. She put her arms around me and held me through my pain. My husband offered a wise anecdote. He compared my situation to one of an athlete who has suffered an injury. *Would a baseball player jump into full play immediately, or would he gently work his way back into the game until fully recovered?*

I've had to take a new approach to life-one of temperate respect for the talents God has given me. *"Come to me, all of you who are weary and carry heavy burdens, and I will give you rest."* Matthew 11:28. God knew I needed to be still for a while. He wanted me to lay down the burden of my concerns and to rest in the certainty that my talents were given to me for my good and for God's glory. Meanwhile, I'm actually learning to *enjoy* being quiet, and I'm sure everyone else is enjoying it, too.

(3)

"From the depths of despair, O lord, I call for your help. Hear my cry O Lord. Pay attention to my prayer. I am counting on the Lord; yes, I am counting on him. I have put my hope in his word." Psalms 130:1,2 and 5.

Making marriage work can be one of the most difficult challenges any two people can undertake. It wasn't long before Hallie began to realize her union was going to be a long and difficult road. She had tremendous expectations, and so did Spencer. Neither of them could live up to the lofty ideals of one another. Hallie was a romantic, in need of attention, affection and kind words. Spencer was a man who never saw or experienced this kind of behavior, as he was growing up. Consequently, he was clueless as to her needs. Their approach to problem solving was antagonistic. Hallie is a kind of in-your-face type person. She wants to get everything out on the table and deal with it. Spencer is a pull back, no conflict kind of guy. It seemed impossible to resolve their differences with such diverse approaches to basic communication.

They were headed swiftly down a dark tunnel with no light in sight. After years of struggle, intimacy was virtually non-existent. There was very little closeness between them on any level-spiritual, emotional or physical. The only thing keeping them together was a completely honest and overwhelming devotion to their daughter. Abby was the tiny island of hope in a sea of discontent. They both adored her and wanted to give her a secure and loving home with two parents. In order to accomplish this, they simply made a decision to agree to disagree. The reality of this type of situation, it only lasts *so* long. Something has to give, and eventually, everything came unglued. They were battling continually, Hallie, in her boxing gloves, and Spencer against the ropes, each causing the other tremendous pain with their words and actions. She felt it needful to end the marriage, firmly believing there had to be a more loving and hopeful situation available to her than a co-existent union.

Surprisingly, Spencer was not willing to end the marriage, though Hallie couldn't understand his reticence. She was all too aware of his misery over the years. Hallie stood in her kitchen praying a simple prayer. *Lord, you see my heart. You know I want to give and receive love. I want out of this situation before I waste any more precious time. If you have a solution to this, or if you want me to stay, you must show me in some manner. I am completely at my end.*

Two days later in the middle of the afternoon, there came an unexpected knock at the front door. Surprisingly, there stood a clergyman and his wife Hallie had known for years, but had not had any communication with for a long time. The minister's words were simple and to the point. "The Lord woke me in the night and told me to come here. He said you were considering divorce and that he has a better plan for you. He wants your marriage to be successful, and he has sent us to help you."

Hallie stood speechless at the door, unable to move. Spencer stepped up behind her and saw the couple waiting for an answer. "Come in and sit down," he requested. They knew their divorce discussions had been kept confidential. Only their closest friends knew they were having some problems, and even the friends were unaware of the magnitude. There was no physical way this clergyman and his wife could have had knowledge of Hallie and Spencer's intentions. And yet, here they were, ready to intervene. Had God really heard her prayer?

As soon as they took their seat on the sofa in the living room, the man opened his *Bible* and began to share scripture about God's love and his plan for marriage. He looked directly at Hallie and Spencer and said, "God has seen you sitting in the floor with piles of bills surrounding you, desperately trying to resolve your financial dilemma. He has heard every argument the two of you have shared. He knows both of your dreams, goals and desires. If you will not get in a hurry here, we can walk through these issues, step by step. It will be difficult, and it will be painful at times, but God wants to heal the wounded parts of your heart that you have hidden from each other. There is tremendous pain you brought into the marriage that neither one of you are aware of. God will bring all this to light, if you are willing; and when he is finished, you will have something strong to build the rest of your lives upon. Is this a direction you both want to go?"

Hallie and Spencer both looked at each. Tears were in his eyes. Spencer's prideful walls were crumbling with the mere knowledge of God's great love for them. *Why did God care so much?* They neither one could speak; however, they nodded their heads affirmatively.

The clergyman began to unfold their secrets before them like a dark and sorrowful book-a piece of literature no one would want to read, a play no thespian would choose to perform. At every revelation there was a time for prayer, tears and reflection. The couple stayed with Hallie and Spencer that day for several hours and offered to meet with them weekly for as many weeks, or months, as were necessary to complete the work God was beginning in them that day.

Over the counseling sessions that followed, Hallie began to understand that in her own self-involved way, she had completely over-looked the suffering Spencer was going through, her own depression clouding her ability to see his pain. Each session brought them to a new level of compassion for each other, previously untouched. They had erroneously viewed one another as strong, independent individuals without need, without vulnerability; when in fact; they were both little children, desperate for affirmation and loving-kindness.

The process was difficult. Sometimes the pain was more than either of them could bear. Digging through the past with all its hidden heartache was no picnic. There were days they felt the burden of their mistakes and wondered if they could actually come to a place of acquittal for each other. However, once Hallie and Spencer understood what they needed from the relationship and had taken the time to receive healing in the various areas of past wounds, they were both anxious to begin again. This time they stepped forward with clear direction and resolve to take care of one another, and protect each other's hearts and lives.

As Hallie and Spencer faced the road together, they began to see a bit of light at the end of the tunnel. With each session the illumination grew brighter, and by the end of the year, they were coming out of a very dark pit into a day filled with hope for a brighter future.

The verse at the beginning of this expository describes perfectly the feelings of hopelessness. *"From the depths of despair, O Lord, I call for your help. Hear my cry, O Lord. Pay attention to my prayer."* Psalms 130:1, 2. The Lord indeed heard Hallie's prayer. He *felt* their pain. He understood their needs better than they did. He repaired Spencer's heart, as well as Hallie's. His love reached into a desperate situation with hope, benevolence and reconciliation. He turned their sorrow into *dancing-beyond depression.*

(4)

"Elijah went to Beersheba, a town in Judah, and he left his servant there. Then he went on alone into the desert, traveling all day. He sat down under a solitary broom tree and prayed that he might die. 'I have had enough, Lord,' he said. 'Take my life, for I am no better than my ancestors.'" I Kings 19:3b-4.

The cell phone was beeping, and Sierra had a feeling she knew who was calling as she stood holding the garage door open for the wayward dog. Making a mad dash for the kitchen she answered, irritated and out of breath. "Hello?"

"Hey, Babe, how's it going?" Tim, as usual, was away on business and called whenever the mood struck him. "I hope this isn't a bad time."

"Are you kidding? I finally rounded up Rascal after a mid-night rendezvous with the neighborhood dalmatian, and the kids are just coming in the door from school-just the predictable bedlam around here. When are you coming home?"

"Well, that's what I want to talk to you about." *Oh brother, what's he cooked up now?*

"I want you to keep an open mind and check out the e-mail I've just sent you." Call me after you take a look."

"No hair-brained ideas, please-I don't have the energy."

After home-work, piano lessons, soccer practice, and cleaning up the dinner dishes, Sierra collapsed, exhausted in a heap in front of the lifeless computer, a mirror image of her emotions. After the necessary adjustments, Tim's e-mail popped up.

Don't jump to conclusions. Just open the attachments and take a look at the opportunity. Sierra clicked on the icon and gorgeous views of the ocean in its panoramic splendor greeted her weary eyes. At the bottom a single sentence followed. *Wouldn't you love to live here?* Sierra leaned back in her chair, pushed the keyboard away and sat staring at the ocean. *He can't be serious.*

In the days and weeks to come, Tim's intentions became clear. He was intensely focused on relocation. Everyday found her more and more panicked over the possibility of such a huge upheaval. Her work was here, her teaching, her family and friends. Everything she knew and loved was five minutes in any direction. *Why would he do this to me?*

Before Sierra could calculate her loss, she found herself packing up their belongings and making the long trek to the unknown world of sunshine and blue oceans. *I must be out of my mind.* Having sold the house with very little equity, they were without the financial means to purchase another. The family settled into a nice little apartment in the heart of the city. At first, it all seemed vacation-like; Sierra's mind not comprehending this as a permanent change. However, as the weeks became months, her heart longed for the friends and family she left behind. The household chores were becoming more and more difficult to complete. The children were irritating her in ways they had never before. She knew no one in this place and didn't really care to make new friends. *We've got to move back home.*

Tim's business was taking off, skyrocketing in fact. He was so busy with his new opportunity; he didn't seem to notice Sierra's despondency. The kids were doing well, the home was tidy, all a reflection of an orderly family. He knew Sierra was struggling, but he tried not to make too much of it. *She'll work through this in time.*

One evening, Tim came into an apartment overrun with toys and clothes. Nothing was prepared for dinner, and the kids were running wild. Sierra was lying on the bed staring motionless at the grey ceiling. "What's going on here? Everything is a mess. Are you sick?" Tim's question was met with a marked silence. He stepped over to where Sierra was lying and bent down on one knee. "Babe, what's the matter. What can I do?"

"I don't want to be here, anymore. Take me home where I belong. The vacation is over," Sierra replied with stoic resolve.

"Sierra, honey, we *live* here. This isn't a vacation. This is our new home. I know the apartment is small, nothing like the house we used to have, but trust me. The company is doing well, and it's just a matter of time before we can buy our own home and settle in."

"I don't want to settle in, Tim. I want to go home."

"This *is* home now, Sierra."

"Who do you think you are, to take me away from everything I loved? My work was fulfilling, my friends were supportive, and my family helped me with the kids. Mom even walked Rascal when I needed. Here I have no one, Tim. No one is here to help me do anything. I am completely alone, and I'm miserable."

Tim sat on the side of the bed studying the teary face of the woman he loved. He knew this was going to be a tough call, but their financial future rested on his decision. He simple couldn't make a decent living in the previous situation. The opportunity to start his own business with a terrific partner was something he couldn't pass up. The company was doing so well, Tim hadn't taken the time to notice Sierra's broken heart; perhaps he didn't want to notice.

"You're right, Babe. This was selfish of me. You already know all the reasons we had to come here. But, if you want to go back home for a time and visit, then I will make the necessary arrangements. In fact, anytime you want to go home and see everyone, we'll find a way for you to do that. But Sierra, it's time to get out of this apartment and start meeting people. I want you to promise me, you will make an effort to find some new friends. Can you do that for me?"

Sierra studied Tim's worried face, and she knew he was more fulfilled than she'd ever seen him before. He was literally thriving with this new company, and he had found a place where his talents were utilized to their fullest. *Could she possibly do the same?*

◆◆

Depression can immobilize and blind us to life's tremendous possibilities. We can plant a dense forest of denial so protectively around our heart, nothing can get in. Consequently, nothing can get out either. All the anger, frustration and self-pity consume us, until we lose sight of the possibilities that await us.

Poor Elisha in the opening scripture of this segment was also uprooted from the familiar and felt an overwhelming sense of despair. He went so far as to pray that he might die. It's a good thing God can see past our trauma-filled moments to a brighter day and carefully weighs our prayers before answering. Elisha reached out in desperation to the heart of a listening God and heard the gentle whisper of compassion that offered him both insight and direction for his future.

Fortunately for Sierra, she made the willful choice to reach beyond the boundaries of melancholy, and grasp hope with both hands and a determined heart. It took months for her to find her place in this new life, but she did make good friends, while maintaining close contact with the previous ones, and began working on her projects with renewed vigor. The move enriched her life in ways she never dreamed possible and added fresh perspective to her creative abilities. *Who could possibly find fault with painting at the sea-shore?*

God always knows what we need. Many of his decisions are initially disagreeable to our natural need for consistency. However, sometimes deviation is necessary to propel us in directions God desires we go. His plans are far above ours, and his ways are often strange to our human sense of accord. However, he is keenly aware of our needs and our talents, and he knows what it will take to bring our very best qualities to the forefront. God has this wonderful way of turning our depression into an opportunity for growth and maturity, if we will only allow him.

(5)

"So now there is no condemnation for those who belong to Christ Jesus." Romans 8:1.

Not every job results in bonuses and promotions. Not every friendship survives the complications of life. Not every marriage makes it for the long haul.

Libby, a great friend I've known for years, has been married as long as I have. She's got a wit as sharp as a carving knife and a laugh that stops you dead in your tracks. Her self-depreciating humor is rollicking, and she is never without an interesting story to tell. That's why it was shocking to hear her say these words.

"After much soul searching, I've come to realize Gary and I are not going to make it. There is no one else involved-no affairs or dark secrets. I simply can't make him see what I need. Just a dinner reservation or a thoughtful word could turn this all around. He thinks I'm being silly when I request some small kindness. He considers me a spoiled wife with little to do but sit around and think of things to complain about. I've tried to convey my feelings, but he won't listen. He rolls his eyes and walks out the door."

"Can't you both go see a counselor and try to get an unbiased and objective viewpoint?" I asked, incredulously.

"It won't matter. We've been down that road before, and it only helped temporarily. Within months we were right back in the same negative groove. Gary doesn't see his need to change. He has a mindset that is unmovable and non-negotiable. As long as I do what is required, everything is fine. But as soon as I express my feelings or needs, he puts up the emotional roadblocks and walks away leaving me completely alone."

I knew Libby had given her marriage her full attention and effort, but her husband simply couldn't grasp the longing inside her heart for love and tenderness. She had been his bookkeeper, business partner, and the mother of his children. *What more could she possibly want?*

Men and women are profoundly different. God made us this way to complete us. He gives men to women for the security of a strong arm. He allows them to take the lead in order to clear the path for us with their powerful machete. And yet, sometimes it's their strength that stands in the way of their vulnerability. How can they be stalwart and still provide sensitivity and kindness? He gives women to men so they will stop and smell the roses of life. He uses women to help men understand the need for simplicity and intimacy. Together, both respecting each other's unique gifts, a couple can be invincible.

Libby made many efforts over the years to repair the damaged relationship and set sail on a new course, but *both* people must want to steer the ship. One party preparing the rigging while the other stands disinterested on the shore doesn't produce a successful journey.

I genuinely believe that *most* relationships are salvageable with willingness, dedication, and outside help. It was difficult for me to step back and accept that Libby's decision was indeed her prerogative. I focused on being a good listener, a good friend, and someone she could trust to talk and pray with.

Life goes on. God understands our needs and our hearts, and does not condemn us for choices we make. I have every certainty that God desires our marriages to work. I also believe his heart is grieved when we divorce. However, I'm certain if he could forgive the numerous biblical characters that made *notable* blunders, God can, and will forgive us. The ever-important issue is to be certain our hearts are right with our Creator. If we ask for his absolution of our errors and make the effort to move forward with a life that pleases him, we can work through the pain, guilt and condemnation associated with a failed union. *So now there is no condemnation for those who belong to Christ Jesus.* Romans 8:1.

I had an elderly friend many years ago whose wise proverbs sustained me during difficult times. He had this amazing way of putting life's challenges into perspective. He'd often say with a grin, "Remember Dear, the world keeps turning. Tomorrow is another day. Tomorrow will be better." I loved him for that. And, I was quick to pass his sage counsel on to my dear friend, Libby.

Tomorrow *is* a better day for those of us who put our faith in a loving Savior and Lord who cares about our pain and suffering. He doesn't condemn us, and we shouldn't condemn ourselves.

(6)

"He was despised and rejected, a man of sorrows, acquainted with bitterest grief. We turned our backs on him and looked the other way when he went by." Isaiah 53:3.

When giving examples of depression, who better to demonstrate than Jesus, the Christ? Who better to serve as our role model for victorious living? Here was a man people were drawn to, but repelled by at the same time. The Spirit within him drew the hardest of hearts to repentance (godly change), and yet his closest companions betrayed him. Jesus saw the true nature of men and still loved them. He knew the treacherous ways common to humanity, and still felt compassion. Those he loved most had difficulty understanding him, and some dismissed his life and his teachings. His own disciples, men he trained and spent time with, turned away from him in his darkest hour of need. He was completely displaced-a heavenly spirit trapped in an earthly body. He felt pain, sorrow, rejection, and loneliness. In spite of all this, Jesus lived a sinless life, above reproach-full of integrity, love, and kindness.

Few of us will ever experience pain comparable to the sufferings of Jesus. I doubt we will ever know what it feels like to have crowds of people scorn and ridicule us. If anyone had a perfect right to suffer depression, he did. However, Jesus knew his call. He understood his purpose. He had a relationship with his Father God-one of complete trust, two hearts beating as one. His flesh experienced all the things we feel in order to gain understanding for our sufferings. He is deeply moved by the feelings of our afflictions. He cares about our pain and dejection. Jesus came to apprehend our struggle, taking our burdens on his own back, so we would not have to carry them alone. By exposure to life in human flesh, Jesus could authentically convey our grief, distress, delight, pain, and certainly our fears to his heavenly Father.

Though it would seem the story had a tragic ending, Jesus' greatest victory was established through death. Only in death could he take all the knowledge he had gained on earth back to his Father in heaven. Only in death was he able to pay the ransom on our heads due to sin. We can reach out to Jesus, *knowing* he grasps all the complexities of humanity and is both willing and *able* to bring us through to victory. We never have to face depression or any other malady of human flesh, unaided. We have the resources of heaven at our disposal. All we need to do is *ask.*

Gray skies are gonna clear up,
Put on your happy feet!

Walking in Love

chapter seven

(1)

"If I could speak in any language in heaven or on earth, but I didn't love others, I would only be making meaningless noise like a loud gong or a clanging cymbal. If I had the gift of prophecy, and if I knew all the mysteries of the future, and knew everything about everything, but didn't love others, what good would it be? And if I had the gift of faith so that I could speak to a mountain and make it move, without love I would be no good to anybody. If I gave everything I have to the poor and even sacrificed my body, I could boast about it, but if I didn't love others, I would be of no value whatsoever. Love is patient, love is kind. Love is not jealous, or boastful or proud, or rude. Love does not demand its own way. Love is not irritable, and it keeps no record of when it has been wronged. It is never glad about injustice, but rejoices whenever the truth wins out. Love never gives up, never loses faith, is always hopeful, and endures through every circumstance." I Corinthians 13:1-7.

"Hey Mom, hurry up, I'm gonna be late for the soccer game."

"Yeah, yeah, just give me a minute while I throw this load of wash in," Mom replies.

"Can we stop by the mall on the way so I can buy these great jeans I saw on sale? You know I *need* them, 'cause school is starting next week!" the daughter begs.

"I'll be right there honey, your cat just threw up all over the new rug," Mom moans.

Sound familiar? We spend so much time doing seemingly important things. The days, weeks, and months whip by much

101

like the wind through the leaves of the trees. We don't see it coming, and we don't see it go. Granted, much of what we do is necessary. If we don't work, how will we eat and pay our bills? Who will take care of our homes, cars, yards, and other responsibilities if we don't? The kids have homework, ballgames, and a large assortment of social activities to accommodate.

All of these obligatory and time-consuming tasks can prevent us from recognizing the big picture. Sometimes we confuse all we *do* as an indication of our love. It's almost as though we placate our conscience with the pure multitude of responsibilities we offer in place of our affection.

My expectations of my own task-oriented personality can often take the place of my *demonstration* of love. You know the hugs, kisses and kind words. I have to remind myself of the necessity to express my heart. I love my children fiercely, even when they don't live up to the plans I may design for them. If their choices are not stellar, I still need to let them know how dear they are to me.

I have come to attach great value to the moments I spend with my teenage daughter, just to hold her and listen to her talk—grateful that she's willing to spend time with me. The joy in her face tells me all I need to know. She wants this connection with *me*. The pleasure of gifts, clothes, and other "stuff" can't compare to one-on-one quality time with her.

Why is it we get lost in the doing and hide behind the schedules that so entrap us? When all is said and done, the only thing anyone will remember is our love, or *lack* of it. The world moves too fast, expecting everyone to run in the same swift race. But if we run the race to the finish line and there is no one there to greet us, what do we really have to be proud of?

I recently read a story about a man who spent every possible moment in a quest toward financial success and independence. Robert's days were 12- to 15-hour marathons and every weekend merely an extension of the week. His wife and children stood at the door of his home office with imploring faces and begging hearts, sometimes tearfully expressing their need for time with their dad.

He always made promises, but rarely, if ever, kept them. The boat trips were cancelled, the camping adventures cast aside. Each year, the business monster crept stealthily in and stole more and more of his precious seasons, until one eventful day his oldest son Chad, the clever one, the one most like him, was tragically killed in a car accident. As irony would painfully have it, the accident occurred the same weekend Robert was to have spent fishing with this boy. Again, the weekend was cancelled due to work.

It is incredibly important to take time to touch, speak into, and invest ourselves in the lives of others. Can we be willing to set aside our own agendas long enough to reach the hearts of those we encounter in our daily lives? This is what the above scripture is all about. If we re-evaluate our lives and find our time is consumed in non-personal, non-intimate ventures, it is definitely time to turn the beat around. Rewind the tape and stop the whirlwind of life long enough to develop, re-establish, and nurture relationships that possess eternal benefit. How can we do that?

"But Mom, I'm gonna be late for the soccer game!" the daughter whines. "Sorry, but I gotta have a hug from my wonderful girl before you head out that door!" Mom says, with a smile. Seek a warm embrace today. Tell someone, *"I love you,"* and mean it. Put an affectionate arm around the shoulders of loved ones and comfort them. The only thing we can take with us when we depart this planet is our love for God, affection for others, and acceptance of ourselves. Let's talk about love.

◆◆

The four kinds of love are *agape, phileo, eros,* and *storge.* The first and best known is the Greek word *agape.* This type of love is based on deliberate choice and unconditional resolve. *Agape* is God's kind of love toward us. If we truly *agape* someone, we are far more concerned with their needs and wants than our own. Their welfare is pre-eminent in our thoughts and hearts. This is not a love based on emotion or affection, but *decision.* We don't ask *"What's in this for me?"* But rather, *"How can my life serve yours and bless you in some way?"*

Phileo love is one of affection and friendship. The feelings that go along with *phileo* love are ever changing in intensity. Highs and lows, waves of emotion come and go with *phileo* love. Underlying the changes is a constant affection. A lot of marriages are based on *phileo* love. When the intensity shifts to a less pleasant level, the marriage is thought to be no longer viable. This is why we see a lot of people seeking divorce. There is no resolve or decision to love, but rather the pure affection based on feelings. This is not to say *feelings* are wrong or unimportant, but that they are simply another dimension of love. The strongest relationships we can possibly have are a beautiful weave of both *phileo* and *agape*. Choosing to love unconditionally will naturally bring feelings into play over the course of time. Whether the intensity of emotion is high or low, the decision to love brings solidity and consistency, which is a rewarding outcome.

Eros love is the one most readily accepted and sought after in our society. This love is best described as sexual passion, physical gratification, heat, desire, and arousal. It's a beautiful and wondrous thing between two people who are committed to each other for the long term. Sexual love is more than a binding together of the bodies, but rather a complete connection of the spirit and soul as well. *Eros* love outside of a committed relationship can be a very exciting proposition initially. Let's face it; the desire to be intimate and sexual is an extremely strong force in all of us. However, God knows the importance of respecting this kind of love. We see in the Old Testament of the **Bible** that the sexual act was representative of marriage. Likewise, when someone stepped into an adulterous relationship outside the marriage, God looked on this as a divorce. The spiritual ramifications that go hand-in-hand with *eros* love are profound. We literally become part of someone else's spirit, and they become part of ours when the sexual act is completed. Marriage is the safe haven for *eros* love, and the place God intended it to be for our overall good, spiritually, emotionally and physically.

Lastly, *storge* love refers to the love between families: mother and child, father and child, brother and sister, and all extended parts of this group. The old adage "blood is thicker than water" is a perfect description of the *storge* kind of love. The tie that binds people together through their common family roots is *storge* love.

Hopefully, all of us will experience these four types of love. God's essence encompasses them all, understands them all, and has planned them all to benefit and bless our lives. If we can honor the importance of love, lining up our plans and hopes with God's word, and taking *time* for love, we will begin to experience the fullness of all God has in store for us.

(2)

"You have heard that the Law of Moses says, 'love your neighbor and hate your enemy.' But I say love your enemies! Pray for those who persecute you! In that way you will be acting as true children of your Father in heaven. For He gives His sunlight to both the evil and the good and He sends rain on the just and the unjust, too. If you love only those who love you, what good is that?" Matthew 5:43-46a.

Susan once worked on a small-town musical production. She was quite a talent with a wonderful voice and over-the-top stage skills. One of the other girls in the cast suffered from some misplaced insecurities and set about to sabotage her every move. Each time Susan stood to sing, Pamela whispered nasty remarks in the background and giggled, like some silly grade school child. She would intentionally hurl her comments over a live microphone, just loud enough for the audience to hear.

Her abuse was especially calculating in the dressing room. Pamela would unscrupulously hide certain items of clothing in order to make it impossible for Susan to get ready for her next scene. It was absolutely maddening. After months of abuse, Susan was really at her wits end. She prayed for the girl, she prayed for her own sanity, unsuccessfully attempted to open the lines of communication, and finally gave serious thought to quitting the show. She reached out to the director for help, but his advice was despairingly hollow. "Ignore her, she's just jealous. She'll get over this and move on."

But move on, she didn't. After a particularly grueling performance, Pamela came completely unglued and began shouting obscenities at Susan. Amazingly, Susan stood quietly, even stoically, and listened intently to the venom being hatefully spewed her way. Susan allowed Pamela to ventilate all her anger, and when she was through, Susan calmly told her, "Pamela, we both know your anger is not about me. We both know this difficult night was not my fault, and we both understand you are hurting. Why don't you take some time, cool off and let's sit down and work through this if we can."

Tears began to roll down Pamela's cheeks and she collapsed in a heap on the floor, unable to get up. Susan sat down next to her and put her arms around her, but didn't speak a word. After a very long few moments, Pamela turned to her and said through tear-stained cheeks, "You are so right. I know this isn't your fault. I have always wanted the respect and love of my mother, but she died too soon to see my accomplishments. And, I will never be good enough for my dad, no matter what I do. You seem to have everything figured out, and such great support from your family. It's hard to work side-by-side with you day in and out without feeling like I don't measure up. I want to get through this, and I need your help." This transparent dialogue opened the door for many healing conversations to take place between Pamela and Susan, markedly improving their working relationship.

◆◆

Most of us are aware that hurting people *hurt* people. Those with wounded hearts tend to be the ones who lash out and wound others the most. If we can view those who take on the role of "enemy" with love and insightful compassion, it becomes far easier to treat them with kindness. *I say love your enemies! Pray for those who persecute you! In that way you will be acting as true children of your Father in heaven.* Matthew 5:44,45. Knowing people are acting out and making poor judgment calls due to their own pain and negative experiences makes it far easier to accept their human frailty.

When we pray for those who despitefully misuse us, God is brought into the picture. He lifts the burden off our shoulders and begins to work in us and in the one we are having conflict with. We can't change the other guy, but the *real* transformation takes place in our hearts first. Susan gained greater patience than she had ever known, due to this encounter. She was strengthened emotionally while learning to stand in integrity in the midst of a very trying circumstance.

When we take the time to look at another person's suffering, we are not so quick to seek revengeful solutions to our difficulties. And, we begin to see the results of God's hand operating in and through the situation.

Prayer coupled with sincere kindness and a desire to love our enemies is a powerful combination. It's one that brings conversion to all situations. Even if we can't see a difference in the other person, we are certainly aware of our internal metamorphosis. Through a willful decision to love, simply making up our minds to love the unlovable, we can have God's peace operating in our hearts. Then the altercations we endure with people who are acting out from a point of pain, still result in a positive outcome for us. Love is an awesome and life changing force. God smiles at us when we make the effort to love those who mistreat us. I'm still working on this one!

(3)

"O Lord you have examined my heart and know everything about me. You know when I sit down or stand up. You place your hand of blessing on my head. Such knowledge is too wonderful for me, too great for me to know! You made all the delicate inner parts of my body and knit me together in my mother's womb. Thank you for making me so wonderfully complex! Your workmanship is marvelous and how well I know it. You watched me as I was being formed in utter seclusion, as I was woven together

in the dark of the womb. You saw me before I was born. Every day of my life was recorded in your book. Every moment was laid out before a single day had passed." Excerpts from Psalms 139.

I vividly recall the birth of my daughter. Nine months had not prepared me for the overwhelming wonder of holding this tiny person in my arms for the first time. I painstakingly went over every inch of her little body in complete astonishment at the perfection of her being. I felt an odd sense of connection, a sensation completely foreign to me and warmth in my heart previously unknown. My mother and aunt stepped quietly into the room immediately following her birth, and the look on their faces gave me such a sense of thankfulness for what God had just done for my husband and me. My aunt commented on how blessed I was to have this little child to hold and love. She was unable to have children of her own and readily helped raise my little cousins. The longing in her face will always be embedded in my memory.

From that moment my world would never again be the same. Like a rose unfolding its petals and fragrance, so my heart began to welcome this new sensation of overwhelming love. I could not get enough of her. I wanted to hold her every second. My mom finally convinced me she needed some crib time and I needed some rest. The bond forming between this precious little girl and me was undeniably tangible. Every little noise she made in the night roused me from my bed of half-sleep to her crib. Those little toes and fingers were constantly kissed without resistance, and the trusting look in those beautiful brown eyes melted me like chocolate on a warm day. Her smell, that delicious baby smell, was addicting. I had to rub my nose in her hair every time I picked her up. What a change had come over me. The self-involved, overly ambitious, get-ahead kind of gal turned into this big, mushy bag of sugar.

The revelation of God's love for me and for all his creation became suddenly clear. My heavenly Father knew me in my mother's womb as he also knew my child prior to her birth. There is no greater love than the love God has for his creation. We are the fortunate recipients of this gift. God's great and awesome devotion for us was set into motion before we took our first breath. His absolute knowledge of our shortcomings, failures, and self-consumed existence in no way deters his ardor for his children. He loves us still; much in the same way I love my baby girl. Love that realizes weakness and inadequacy and yet embraces without doubt or hesitation is perfect love.

As we learn to trust God much in the same way our children trust us, through day-to-day experiences, we begin to grasp some definitive clarity as to the magnitude of his love and responsibility toward us. As we reach our hearts toward God in faithful devotion, he pours his love into us-much like liquid poured into a cup. The more we reach toward the ultimate source of tenderness, the fuller our cups become. The more we love our children, the more they are drawn into the warmth of our affection.

"O Lord you have examined my heart and know everything about me. You saw me before I was born. Every day of my life was recorded in your book. Every moment was laid out before a single day had passed." Psalms 139. There is tremendous comfort in this beautiful text. Just as my little girl was comforted in my loving embrace, so I can trust my heavenly Father will hold me safe in his arms of tender affection and guide my life to the fulfillment of its destination.

(4)

"And have you entirely forgotten the encouraging words God spoke to you, His children? He said, 'My child, don't ignore it when the Lord disciplines you, and don't be discouraged when He corrects you. For the Lord disciplines those He loves, and He punishes those He accepts as his children.' As you endure this divine discipline, remember that God is treating you as His own children. Whoever heard of a child who was never disciplined? If God doesn't discipline you as He does all of his children it means that you are illegitimate and are not really His children after all. Since we respect our earthly fathers who disciplined us, should

we not all the more cheerfully submit to the discipline of our heavenly Father and live forever?" Hebrews 12:5-9.

Sharon was a pretty good kid growing up. She rarely got into trouble, and for the most part was obedient to her parent's wishes. However, there was one memorable day when Sharon learned a valuable lesson.

In the fourth grade, she walked to and from school each day. It was only a short stroll of three or four tree-lined blocks, so Sharon's parents were comfortable with her little journey. This fine day, she made a decision to go the opposite way from her house to visit her dear Aunt Norma. She was the only woman in the world Sharon loved to be around as much as her own mother. So without informing her parents of her plan, she found a buddy from her class and headed to the BelAir subdivision. When she arrived at Auntie's house, they immediately began baking cookies and braiding hair. Sharon's Aunt assumed she had cleared the visit with her parents, but such was not the case. About an hour and a half into their playtime Aunt Norma became suspicious Sharon had acted without their knowledge. She suggested a call to the parents would be appropriate-just to make sure they knew her whereabouts.

Mom and Dad had *no* idea where she was, had already called the police, and alerted the entire neighborhood to Sharon's disappearance. She was in some *serious* trouble. She had no understanding as to the magnitude of their alarm until she saw the look of overwhelming relief on their faces as she arrived home. Mother swept her up in her arms and cried. Dad stood staring at Sharon's blonde braids; almost disbelieving she was actually standing in the living room. They had spent the last two hours imaging the most frightening things.

Needless to say, her father's relief quickly turned to anger when he realized how thoughtless Sharon had been. With deft resolve he took her into the back bedroom, picked up the little wooden paddle, and applied some discipline to her seat of learning. Sharon's father did not *beat* her; he was controlled, quick, and to the point. The only thing painful about the punishment was the knowledge she had disappointed her parents. Sharon *never* forgot that lesson. She never went to Auntie's house or anywhere else again without permission. This was a lesson well learned.

Looking back on those years, it is so clear to see how dearly Sharon's parents loved their little girl. They didn't want anything to happen to her. They wanted her to make good decisions and began their discipline at an early age to help direct her path on a course of excellence. She is and will always be eternally grateful for their love, devotion, and correction.

Likewise, some of us have had some pretty intense disciplinary sessions with our Heavenly Father. You may wonder how God can train us, but it is not so unlike the experiences we have with loving parents. When we make decisions that are contrary to the leading of our heart, we usually pay the price for our obstinacy.

◆◆

It was the day before Thanksgiving. The air was crisp and cold. My best friend Elise and I decided a quick jaunt to the city for some intense Christmas shopping was in order. We talked for weeks about the trip and saved our money, dutifully. We carefully selected our wardrobe as one can't shop unless one looks fabulous. We met early that day for the two hour trek north. The shopping was the motive, but teenage girls need no particular reason to search out adventure. My little car was adequate for the journey, and we made it to our destination without mishap. We shopped till we dropped and headed to the home of my lovely aunt and uncle to spend the night. The next morning, the sky looked dark and a bit foreboding. The clouds had a threatening color of grey, and they were creeping ominously closer. I felt a small but certain warning to simply pack up the car and head home. Elise felt it, too. However, the stores were beckoning seductively, and there were a few more items still not purchased on the Christmas lists. So off we went to the mall for just a couple of browsing hours before the journey home.

When we came out, we knew we were in trouble. Snow was falling in a dense cloud and the streets were already white, ripe with accumulation. While we were oblivious, the world was evolving from fall to winter. Truly it was beautiful, but sometimes the loveliest things are the most dangerous.

We had a quick pow-wow to decide if we should head back to the safety and warmth of Auntie's home or try to brave the storm. Thanksgiving turkey and all the trimmings were enticing us to make the journey. Bravely we began, but one block from the mall, my little car went into a tailspin and nearly crashed into the guardrail. We should have taken that incident as a firm warning, but age and immaturity played a large part in our poor decision-making.

Creeping along at 5 to 10 miles per hour, my little car had a tough time staying on the road. We decided the best route would be the smaller, less traveled highway. Repeatedly, we slipped and slid-with the car in the ditch more than on the road. When we had all but given up, kind truckers took pity on us and let us follow behind as they plowed the road ahead.

After several harrowing experiences, lots of screams, numerous tears, and repeated prayers, we finally arrived safely back home to the relief of frantic parents. Twelve long hours had passed since our fateful decision to venture out into that storm.

◆◆

The still, small voice God places in our hearts is there for an important reason. I have experienced the benefits lavished on my life for obedience to God's voice and his word. I have also suffered terribly for ignoring the intuition of my conscience, much like I did in the snowstorm. In the opening verse of this segment, the scripture states that *God disciplines those he loves*. Many times that discipline is manifested in the outcome of our rebellion. If only we would listen to that *wise whisper*, we could save our friends, our families, and ourselves a great deal of unnecessary trauma.

We are fortunate when we have the experience of loving discipline in our lives. In dealing with our own children, we can experientially tap into the wisdom and tolerance demonstrated by both God and parent. Though we don't always enjoy the corrections that result in our defiance, whether from our Heavenly Father or our earthly attendants, we certainly *learn* from them. And, we become better people in the loving disciplinary process.

By the way, that little spanking Sharon's dad gave her in the fourth grade was the first and the *last*.

A song in your heart puts a
spring in your step!

Rebounding From Rejection

chapter eight

(1)

"Samson fell in love with a woman named Delilah, who lived in the valley of Sorek. The leaders of the Philistines went to her and said, 'Find out from Samson what makes him so strong and how he can be overpowered and tied up securely. Then each of us will give you eleven hundred pieces of silver.' So Delilah said to Samson, 'Please tell me what makes you so strong and what it would take to tie you up securely.'" Judges 16:4-6.

It was a lovely clear day in the hills as Samson and his parents made their way down the winding road toward the city. His parents were quite a bit ahead of him on the path, caught up in their conversation. Samson, preoccupied with his own daydreams, was oblivious to the danger stalking in the vineyards nearby.

She had been watching for quite some time, stealing through the high grass, and deftly maneuvering her way in and out of the grapevines, waiting for her opportunity to grasp a quick and easy meal. Slowly she crept until she was only a few feet away from her prey. In an unexpected instant, the lioness was airborne. She pounced with ferocity toward Samson's throat. She would have torn him to bits, but he caught her lunge out of the corner of his eye and met her just as her jaws were poised to close in on the highly anticipated meal. His left hand went around her head, and grasped her bottom jaw. His right hand gripped the back of her top teeth and with one stupendous

114

pull an audible crack resounded through the air. The lioness fell from Samson's arms and landed in a heap as the life drained from her body. He stood looking over her with pounding heart and ragged breath, the first of several encounters in Samson's life that would test his will and his strength.

Not long after his confrontation with the lioness, Samson found himself at odds with his countrymen. The air was tense as the men stood waiting for Samson to emerge from his home. "What is it you want?" Samson asked with a knowing heart.

"We must take you and turn you over to the Philistines, lest they come and destroy us." Samson had a serious run in with the enemies of Israel, and Samson's countrymen were being threatened with war if they didn't turn over their strong hero. Samson studied their troubled faces. *Were they more frightened of the Philistines, or of Samson?* Fear ripped through their bodies like a frozen wind as they glanced over the valley toward the waiting Philistine soldiers.

"We have no choice, Samson. If we don't bring you, they will come down on us and leave our home barren and wasted."

"I want your solemn word you will not kill me, but rather turn me over unharmed to the infidels."

One of the younger and stronger men took Samson's powerful hands and bound them behind his back with new, unused rope of double strength. Samson looked in their eyes with solemn dignity as they escorted him to his fate.

The Philistines were overjoyed at their triumph. They shouted and danced with fervor while Samson was delivered into their hands. As Samson observed their glee, an overwhelming rage began to rise up in his heart, and before they could take hold of their prey, he snapped the ropes in two as if they were a simple string. In one swift fluid motion, he reached down and picked up a donkey's jawbone lying on the ground and came up with a hard right swing. The Philistines were upon him. In a flurry of arms, Samson kept swinging and throwing punches. He was on fire. Every sinew and muscle was charged with super human power. He fought like this for hours, until the Philistines fled in all directions, admitting their defeat. Samson's breathing was labored as he slumped to the ground. Glistening sweat covered his exhausted body. One by one his countrymen, the ones who had turned him over to their oppressors, came out of hiding and stood beside him. No one spoke. They only stared in disbelief at the mayhem spread out before them. One thousand enemy Philistines lay dead in the field, Samson alone their slayer. *Was there no way to defeat him?*

A young Philistine woman took notice of the strongman with the handsome face. She made certain he saw her each time she made her trip to the well. Though it was out of the way for her and water was available much closer to home, she had another purpose in mind. Samson couldn't help but notice her lovely curves and alluring face. The way she looked at him with her veil seductively pushed back over one eye, made his pulse quicken. He couldn't help but follow her back to her home, and without any resistance, he took her for his own.

Delilah was not a woman of virtue or integrity. She simply wanted to conquer the unconquerable. Bragging rights were significant to a woman with very little to boast about. Word got back to Philistine spies concerning Samson's clandestine affair, and swiftly a plan was put to action for his destruction. It was common knowledge Delilah was easily persuaded for financial gain, and she gladly accepted a large sum of money from the enemy leaders. Her assignment? She was hired to discover the source of Samson's great strength.

Each time he made his way to her bed, she inquired of him the secret to his power, and time and time again he made up elaborate stories to placate her inquiries. Finally though, he acquiesced, feeling guilty for lying to the woman he loved and divulged the mystery of his enormous strength.

God promised Samson his strength would be assured providing he never cut his hair. Having entrusted his great secret to the woman he loved, she promptly brought in the barber in the middle of the night, as Samson slept in the comfort of her arms. When he awoke in the morning, he was horrified to see his hair had been shorn, and he was as weak as any other man. Not only was his physical strength gone, but also his heart was broken by Delilah's betrayal. Samson had a double dose of rejection: Delilah's deception and his own betrayal to God's promise, which alienated him from the favor and trust of God's heart.

He was immediately taken to the camps of the enemy, callously tortured, and by the searing heat of hot iron pokers, painfully blinded. Strapped to the wheel of a grain processor, he worked endless days as a prisoner of war. It's unclear how long he lived that way, but I am certain he had a lot of time to think about Delilah's deceit. He had untold hours to dream of his days in the rolling hills of his home, watching the children play and to recall his amazing victories conquering the Philistines. Why had he traded all his gifts for senseless nights with a cunning temptress? He continually pondered his pain and rejection and wondered how he could have been so stupid.

Have you ever been there? Hurt by someone you trusted and imagining all the different ways the chapter could have unfolded? Unfortunately, there is no way to experience life without experiencing rejection. Interpersonal relationships all present the possibility of dismissal. It is completely unavoidable. However, if we can choose instead to find some gain in our disappointments, some reason to hope, some lesson captured, then rejection is not the victor. *We are.*

The ending of Samson's story is in keeping with Old Testament victory. He was brought before the Philistines at festival time, shackled and chained, the enemy trophy for their amusement. The atmosphere was festive as they all ate, drank, and made merry. Many stood and jeered at the man once considered to be an undefeatable foe. Some even threw food at him in their mockery. Though Samson's eyes were unseeing, his ears were keenly attuned to the taunts of his prime adversary. The servants of the Philistine leaders made the ominous mistake of securing Samson to the middle pillars of their great edifice. Samson realized his opportunity and humbly requested God's favor and power to enable him one last time. With God's supernatural strength, Samson placed his hands on the pillars that supported the roof and pushed with all his might. *In the name of Jehovah.* The building began to crumble and people ran screaming in horror as the colossal roof caved in, dropping huge chunks of hardened clay and mortar on all who were trapped inside. No one survived.

This was not only Samson's vindication, but also God's *justice.* Samson was created to be a leader within the tribes of Israel; and in his final hour, he was allowed to be victorious over the enemies of his people. He was again privileged to use the gifts given to him early on, restoring the once intimate relationship between him and his Creator.

◆◆

If we are willing to turn our rejections over to the hand and heart of God, the Holy Spirit, author of liberty, is set free to operate in our hearts and the hearts of those who have caused harm. It's not likely the roof will fall in on our oppressors. However, God has a definitive plan, and he desires that we be whole, not broken. He has infinite knowledge of each time we have been cast aside. He sees every distress we have carefully hidden behind doors of denial. And, he knows with absolute clarity what is needed to free us from the prison of disdain. As long as our heart is bound with chains of scorn, we cannot possibly be free to experience all that life has to offer.

Our God is a skillful healer of the complicated issues of the human heart, but only when we can trust enough to lay them out on the table before him. *Here it is Lord, please begin your conciliatory work in me.* Rebounding from rejection begins with acknowledging the existence of the pain; then realizing God is able to start a life changing work if we request his intervention. He has the divine ability to turn our calamity into advantage. God can take our most intimate rebuff and most calculated mistakes and bring something good from it. I think Samson would agree.

(2)

"As Jesus went with him, he was surrounded by the crowds. And there was a woman in the crowd who had had a hemorrhage for

twelve years. She had spent everything she had on doctors, and still could find no cure. She came up behind Jesus and touched the fringe of his robe. Immediately, the bleeding stopped. 'Who touched me?' Jesus asked. Luke 8:42b-45.

She stepped out into the light of the early morning dawn hoping today would bring resolution to her quest. For twelve long years she had struggled with a malady that had sapped her strength and impaled her spirit. Every doctor available had been hired to cure her, and every saved penny spent in the pursuit of health. Yet she still suffered, completely unable to defeat this formidable foe.

The bleeding never stopped. Sometimes it was less intrusive, other times it was devastating. The energy had slowly drained from her frail body as she made her way through the days. As everyone knew, Jewish law stated a woman during her period was considered to be *unclean.* She could have no physical contact with her family or friends. Her husband was not allowed to have any intimate relations with her. She had to wash in separate basins from everyone else, and if anyone accidentally touched her, they had to go and immediately bathe. Wherever she sat, no one could sit after. All furniture had to be covered lest anyone else suffer her unclean status.

How she longed for human contact. A simple embrace or an understanding look was so desperately needed. None of these were available to someone who was a social castaway, the neighborhood pariah.

Occasionally, she would catch bits of the conversations of her neighbors. *I am staying as far away from her as possible. She must have done something terrible to be punished in this way. Keep your children away from that woman.* The words left deep and painful wounds. However, she knew she was guilty of nothing except a strong and abiding desire to be made whole.

One eventful day Jesus passed by. There were throngs of people pressing in to touch, or be touched, by the Master. His extraordinary reputation for healing the sick preceded him.

Everyone wanted a little piece of him. The woman with the hemorrhage was just another in the crowd of hundreds. Everyone was so taken with Jesus' presence; they weren't paying much attention to the *unclean woman*. They didn't even notice they were bumping into her. They had something remarkable capturing their attention.

Carefully, and as unobtrusively as possible, she edged her way closer and closer, stretching her bony fingers through the throngs of people until she could actually reach the hem of his robe. She knew with absolute certainty she should *not* be touching him. Considering the social order of men and women at this time, her decision was undeniably dangerous.

Her desperation was so great that she was willing to risk everything. And, in that one faith-filled moment as she touched the edge of his clothing with her fragile fingertips, the warmth of his healing power poured through her exhausted body, caressing her wounded spirit, and melting away the years of pain, sorrow, and suffering.

Jesus was suddenly and unerringly aware he had been accessed by faith. *"Who touched me?"* He asked. His disciples, crushed by the huge and desperate crowd, were baffled by his question. And the recipient of his healing power was now kneeling at his feet, trembling with fear, acknowledging her act. The eyes of the crowd were accusingly upon her as they began to recognize this unclean woman, now aware they had been rubbing shoulders with her. Moments before they could not care less who she was. Now all eyes were upon her, the familiar look of disdain and repulsion filling their faces. How utterly terrified she must have been.

There were probably others who were healed that day through the power of his presence. Jesus could have let it go. Why did he single her out for recognition of her act? He was keenly aware of Jewish law. He knew she was a complete social exile. He knew she had risked death to touch him. So he let her explain before the unforgiving crowd gathered that day, her pain and suffering over the past twelve years. He let her tell of her rejection. And, he allowed her to disclose her desperation for all to hear. In this simple act of compassion, Jesus healed not only her physical disorder, but ensured her emotional health. Who would believe she had been healed otherwise? How could she possibly have proven it? By allowing her that moment of transparency before her family and neighbors, the affirmation of Jesus' unqualified acquittal ensured her social standing in the community. No longer would she be bound by the insufferable weight of rejection.

What love the Savior has for his people. Jesus took her suffering then, just as he does for us today. By his death on the cross, the law dissolved and grace took its place. Now, we can come with complete assurance and lay our broken hearts at the feet of Jesus and receive his healing love and restoration for our battered and rejected lives. We can be restored with the same measure of compassion he showed for the woman in the above story. The requirement? A simple act of faith.

(3)

"Jesus entered Jericho and made his way through the town. There was a man there named Zacchaeus. He was one of the influential Jews in the Roman tax-collection business, and he had become very rich. He tried to get a look at Jesus, but he was too short to see over the crowds. So he ran ahead and climbed a sycamore tree beside the road, so he could watch from there. When Jesus came by, he looked up at Zacchaeus and called him by name. "Zacchaeus!" he said, "Quick, come down! For I must be a guest in your home today."
Luke 19:1-5.

Short by most standards, over-weight, balding and certainly not a man possessing any notably attractive physical characteristics, Zacchaeus was an unscrupulous shyster who pictured himself an up and coming entrepreneur. He made himself virtually indispensable to the Roman tax gathering operation with his clever manipulation of currency, all the while taking far more than his fair share from his own people. He made no apologies about his line of work, and without regard, reveled in his outlandish lifestyle. I imagine he smiled every time he over-charged someone, knowing he could buy some new piece of land, herd of sheep, or extravagant luxury for his own pleasure. People in the community despised him, fully aware of his calculated deceit. Everywhere he went he was the scornful subject of the town gossip mill. *Look at that little cheat. He doesn't care about anyone but himself.* Zacchaeus heard their remarks, and in those rare moments of transparency, he would admit to the bitter sting they caused him. However, his love for wealth overpowered his desire for esteem.

The day Jesus passed by resembled many others. People were busy doing their daily work. The market was full of the smell of dust and sweat, fruits and vegetables. Merchants were shouting at potential customers, rallying for their business. The noise of clacking pottery and clinking coins filled the air. Zacchaeus was busily counting his money, separating the Roman's share, and pocketing more than his. Suddenly, people were chattering excitedly and darting about, attempting to get a look at this man from Nazareth. Zacchaeus was no different. He was a curious individual who had by this time heard quite a lot concerning Jesus. He attempted to see him; pushing his way through the crowd, but got elbowed out of the way each time he made an effort to catch a glimpse. No one in this community would go out of his or her way to accommodate Zacchaeus. Being an enterprising fellow, he decided his best recourse was to climb the nearest tree. This was suitably the highest elevation this man had ever attained.

His tenacity was rewarded. Jesus glanced up into the bright sunshine passing through the leaves of the tree and noticed a diminutive man perched precariously on one of the thicker branches. More than a little bemused over the situation, Jesus called him by name, though they had never met, and proceeded to request accommodations in Zacchaeus' home. Imagine the tax collector's amazement when this well-known celebrity acknowledged him!

The townspeople were clearly offended at Jesus' choice of dinner companionship. They whispered among themselves, "Why would this holy man get entangled with a useless swindler? There is far more suitable lodging for a man of his standing." However, Jesus' eyes were focused intently on the little man before him, and the comments of the townspeople were ignored, disregarded for a greater plan.

After a short while in Jesus' presence, the plump, short, balding Jewish fellow was quite changed. Oh, not from the outside. He still looked like the devious chap everyone knew and hated. But his heart of deceit had been turned to a heart of sincerity. He felt true conviction over his dishonest gain, and he genuinely wanted to be accepted and thought well of within his own community. He made a willful and bold proclamation to amend his ways. His unethical path turned to a road of integrity. The villain became a hero, recast from the inside out.

The people were understandably skeptical as to Zaccheaus' transformation, but decidedly hopeful of a genuine change. Time alone would prove the heart of Zacchaeus. And since there is no further mention of his previously naughty behavior, one can assume his metamorphosis was complete.

In a moment, Jesus took all Zacchaeus' hidden pain resulting from his poor choices and created a man complete, whole and honest, willing to amend his ways with gusto.

Only when we meet our maker heart-to-heart, spirit-to-spirit, can we be truly changed. He alone has that amazing ability to recreate something wonderful out of our ruins, rejuvenating the most tattered soul. I'm appreciative Jesus called Zacchaeus out of that tree, turning his dismissal to approval. It gives us all a wonderful sense of hope.

(4)

"And I am convinced that nothing can ever separate us from his love. Death can't, and life can't. The angels can't, and the demons can't. Our fears for today, our worries about tomorrow, and even the powers of hell can't keep God's love away. Whether we are high above the sky, or in the deepest ocean, nothing in all creation will ever be able to separate us from the love of God that is revealed in Christ Jesus our Lord." Romans 8:38-39.

"Why isn't my shirt ironed? You know I needed that for my appointment today. It was a simple request, but you just can't seem to pull it together, can you?"

"Don, please don't yell at me. I have had my hands full with the kids and the housework. I'm sorry about your shirt. Just hand it to me, and I'll iron it right now."

"Forget it. There's no time for that. I'll be late for my meeting, just like the last time." Pat flinched as the door slammed. She was becoming accustomed to that dreadful sound these days. Each time he walked into the house, she jumped- her stomach in knots, and her heart pounding. *No one should live in fear in their own home.*

Pat's husband was not a man given to kind words and affection. He had strong roots of anger, like an old tree, its tentacles plunged deep into the ground, unmovable. His rage prevented him from displaying any tenderness toward her. He was intensely driven to succeed as if he had something desperate to prove, and his tremendous focus toward his career disconnected him from the intimacy needed to maintain a fruitful marriage. He was incredibly demanding, as well, expecting all household duties to be performed without fail and dinner to be perfectly timed. As Pat attempted to function in a manner acceptable to him, she found her failures mounting. This constant scrutiny began to take its toll on her self-esteem. She cared less and less about her own well being and turned her energies toward her children. However, she needed desperately to know she was acceptable. And after years of criticism and disdain she was dying a slow death, much like a flower left in the hot sun, baked and dry. Pat was in desperate need of some soft and gentle rain.

Don was not intentionally degrading her; he simply didn't like himself very much. People who don't have an understanding of self-appreciation cannot love others. He really didn't know why he was so miserable, but every day was the same. He raged out the door in the mornings and stormed back in it at night. His tremendous insecurities tormented him continually, and in order to survive, he deflected much of his own personal contempt toward Pat and his children. On rare occasion, she would catch a glimpse of the man she knew he could be. The light at the end of the tunnel would appear now and again, and this little ray of hope kept her along for the journey.

Infrequently, Don would do something thoughtful. He would hold the door open, or introduce her to others as his *pretty wife.* None of these things went unnoticed by Pat, so desperate for any small kindness. However, his emotional struggles presented genuine intimacy issues, and Don was completely unable to open his heart to her. For the two of them to share meaningful camaraderie was like trying to penetrate a concrete wall with a sewing needle.

Over the years, as withdrawal and rejection overran any hope for reconciliation, her heart slowly began to harden and become cold and indifferent. After a long run of repeated dismissals, she finally gave up on the optimism that held her in the relationship. Even the tiny rays of hope weren't enough anymore. She honestly believed there had to be *someone* out there who could love her in the ways she needed to be loved. Pat's desire, much like the desire of us all, was to be cherished and appreciated.

The man approached Pat in the grocery store as she was contemplating the size of the Ranch dressing bottle. She couldn't even remember his question. His eyes were so kind and as blue as the sea. He casually touched her arm as he walked away. Everything dead inside her suddenly came to life. A fresh, fragrant wind had just blown through Pat's life, and she wanted more. She waited at the end of the aisle until she saw him checking out in lane four. Quickly she moved her cart in behind his.

"What did you decide on?" she asked shyly. The man smiled with warmth that melted the cold, protective covering around her needy heart.

"How about we grab a cup of coffee, and I'll tell you." He replied.

The days with the man were a constant affirmation of her intelligence and beauty. The intimate moments assured her of her sensuality and feminine allure. For months she saw him when the children were in school, or when her girlfriend was willing to cover for her. Pat was ominously aware of her situation and the danger it posed both to her marriage and her family. She couldn't pray any more. What was the use? God wouldn't listen to a woman willingly stepping into adultery. *Would he?*

There was one constant that kept her from completely disintegrating during that painful time; the childhood training she received regarding the love of God. *"And I am convinced that nothing can ever separate us from his love. Our fears for today, our worries about tomorrow, even the powers of hell can't keep God's love away."* Romans 8. She read and reread the books of Psalms, and Proverbs. She desperately wanted to know God still cared about her, even in the middle of her situation. Somehow this brought her a level of much-needed comfort. God's love was not predicated on her performance, her looks, her intelligence, or any other variable. God's love was completely unconditional, and it was her saving grace.

"Whether we are high above the sky, or in the deepest ocean, nothing in all creation will ever be able to separate us from the love of God that is revealed in Christ Jesus our Lord." Romans 8. She held onto that passage of scripture as though it were a life preserver in a turbulent sea. Pat knew no one would ever love her like God. She found safety within the confines of those scriptures, and protection from the cruelties of human nature. Here was a quiet room she could step into, shut the door, throw away the key, and no one could find her or hurt her.

However, she couldn't hide forever, and the day of facing her situation loomed ominously before her. After carefully weighing her options, Pat finally threw in the towel and decided to seek a divorce. But God had a different plan in mind. He stepped in with his divine form of intervention and began to reveal to Pat and Don the way toward the path of reconciliation.

Pat realized she had to give up the affair in order to take a serious look at her marriage. It was difficult to walk away from someone responsible for the retrieval of her self-esteem, but there was a family to consider and promises to keep. The road to healing was a long and tedious one as the wounds of the human heart go deep, requiring tender medicine to mend. But, Don was willing to examine his past and deal with the wounds of his childhood in order to successfully learn to love without condition or requirement. Pat was agreeable to start anew and address her insecurities and self-esteem issues as well. All these components were necessary in order to begin the process of restoring and healing their broken marriage. With much guidance, excellent counsel, a lot of patience, and a decision to move forward, they started their walk toward the road of restoration.

Imagine peeling the layers of an onion, and you have an excellent picture of their journey. Each layer revealed a new wound requiring attention. Each level brought to light past hurts. As we all know, onions are notorious for their disagreeable scent. As Don and Pat chose the road of honesty rather than denial, the stench of bitterness was unavoidable. However, they painstakingly faced their rejections one-by-one and reconciled their hurtful experiences toward a better end. This was not an easy task. It's doubtful Pat or Don would ever be able or willing to endure the process again. But, if you asked whether or not their course was worth the pain, they would say with confidence, *yes!*

Pat learned to stop hiding her suffering behind a wall of self-pity and to speak up when she felt wounded and condemned. Don learned to express love for his wife in a tangible and affectionate way. He learned to give her praise, and compliments, rather than criticism and cruelty. They have both grown into a new maturity in their relationship with each other, and in their walk with God. All is not picture perfect, but their relationship now maintains the welcome element of *hope*.

◆◆

Rejection can destroy if it is not addressed. We can choose to internalize our pain until we are unable to function as whole, loving beings. This is not God's plan, or his best for his creation. The way *out* is to go *in*. It's important to be honest with feelings of rejection, willing to talk about them. Hidden issues can be devastating, but when exposed to the light of God's love, healing can occur. If we move into God and recognize his unquenchable love for his children, we can grasp hold of the truths in his word, allowing them to be our lifeline. Sometimes it's necessary to boldly reach out to reliable and credible counselors in order to get the help we need.

Father, don't allow us to hide behind walls of pain and rejection. Expose our struggles to the light of your love and mercy in order to bring us to restoration. Heal us from the inside out, as we put our trust and confidence in your great benevolence. Send us the help we need in our troubled hour and surround us with your omnipotent presence as we rest in the knowledge that nothing in all creation will ever be able to separate us from the love of God that is revealed in Christ Jesus our Lord.

(5)

He was despised and rejected-a man of sorrows, acquainted with bitterest grief. We turned our backs on him and looked the other way when he went by. He was despised and we did not care. Yet it was our weakness he carried; it was our sorrows that weighed him down. But he was wounded and crushed for our sins. He was beaten that we might have peace. He was whipped, and we were healed! He was oppressed and treated harshly, yet he never said a word. But who among the people realized that he was dying for their sins-that he was suffering their punishment? Excerpts from Isaiah 53:1-9.

The prophet Isaiah was speaking of events not yet unfolded. He was telling a story through eyes gifted to look beyond the present into the future. With incredible accuracy, Isaiah spoke of the happenings that played out to exacting detail in the life of one man, Yeshua, Jesus the Christ.

If anyone understands our feelings of rejection, Jesus does. If anyone could possibly empathize with our suffering, he could. Not only was he cast aside by his own friends, family and countrymen, but in that one moment when he hung dying on the cross, even God had to look away, as the sin of all mankind, past, present and future, was carried on his shoulders. In my worst distress, I simply cannot imagine his pain.

During the course of his 33 years, he was scorned, ridiculed, and laughed at. He was the misunderstood object of jealousy and disdain. All the while, he continued to teach the good news of God's love; healing, delivering and setting people free from their bondage. Despite insurmountable odds and realizing his destiny, he never stopped loving and giving. Jesus was aware of the price he would have to pay for the sins of mankind. He knew his death (the shedding of innocent blood) was the only atonement for sin. He took the rejection of those around him willingly, knowing his sacrifice was their ultimate hope.

If this assignment had been left to me, the world would surely be lost. There is no way I could have seen past my own pain to sacrificially embrace the needs of others. Certainly not with the same requirement Jesus had to face. But, he bore his rejection with both dignity and grace. The love in his heart for those around him was greater than the pain he suffered at the hands of those who misunderstood him.

There is no one better suited to apprehend our grief and rebuffing. I believe this is why God allowed him to suffer, in order to grasp the depths of our suffering. Thank God we have a high priest that reaches his arms to us in complete comprehension of our trials and struggles. We absolutely never have to face our dilemma alone.

Rejection does not need to be an inconsolable mystery, separating us from the heart of God and the love of those around us. There is no need to hide behind a facade of denial concerning the reality of our pain. We can admit and commit this anguish into the hands of a knowing God, who is fully capable of handling our distress.

In order to rebound from rejection, it helps to:

◆ Admit we are in pain and need assistance in order to recover.

- ◆ Reach out to someone qualified, a clergyman or a therapist, and remain willing to discuss our struggle(s) openly and honestly.
- ◆ Be willing to forgive those who have hurt us with absolute acquittal. This liberates our spirits, allowing us to give and receive love.
- ◆ Request God's divine and omniscient intervention to bring us to the place of freedom he originally designed.

Today is the day. The time is now. Why wait any longer to live a life free and full, rich with the joys God has always intended for those he loves? The time is right to *rebound from rejection.*

Grab the ball and run with it!

Crossing the Sea of Forgiveness

chapter nine

(1)

"If you forgive those who sin against you, (hurt you, misuse you) your heavenly Father will forgive you. But if you refuse to forgive others, your Father God will not forgive your sins." Matthew 6:14-15.

When wounded, some of us have the ability to feign an Oscar-worthy performance, pushing aside our pain and going about our daily business as if nothing happened. Unfortunately, these deeply embedded hurts cannot be ignored. The longer they are suppressed, the deeper the roots of bitterness weave their way through our heart chambers becoming an all-consuming, malignant disease. It stands to reason; the body is seriously impacted by whatever we suffer emotionally and spiritually. Unforgiveness is like a long-term illness of the spirit, gradually invading and infecting every aspect of our lives.

Bitterness is anger that has been left to grow over a long period of time. It slowly hardens our hearts much like an egg left in boiling water for too long. Once a hardening of the heart takes place, the road to forgiveness becomes more difficult. The story below will give an example of the debilitating effects of bitterness.

◆◆

As a small child, Anna's parents owned a skilled care nursing facility. Children were always a welcome diversion to the predictability of life in a structured environment. There was a wonderful woman who lived there and everyone was drawn to her,

Lady Bird Simpson. Curly white hair framed her oval face and the expressive lines on her cheeks and forehead made one envious for the adventurous life clearly written there. Her laugh was contagious and welcoming, like a warm cup of tea on a cold day.

One afternoon Anna and Lady Bird were sitting together on her bed, having yet another of their lovely conversations. Lady Bird began to speak about an old friend of hers, one she knew so well. One she knew so long. He left her when she was young and trusting and made her best girlfriend her worst enemy. Although Anna didn't fully understand the adult content of the story, Lady Bird's pain was clear, even to a child. Her countenance, that lovely warm glow Anna had grown so accustomed to, suddenly changed without warning. *Who is this person sitting beside me?* The suffering etched on Lady Bird's face and the anger so old, yet fresh and new again, distorted this lovely woman into a bitter, scornful old lady.

Anna hesitated to say anything. She was so stunned at the metamorphosis before her. And yet, with the honesty of a child, she proceeded to ask why Lady Bird was so upset. The familiar voice rose in an unfamiliar tone and her eyes narrowed with anger as she exclaimed, *I will never forgive him for what he did to me. Never.*

When pride enters the picture and pronounces the person or circumstance responsible as *unworthy* of our heartache, we begin to tell ourselves we really *don't feel* any pain. After a long period of denial, we begin to believe the lie. We will never grow spiritually if we shelter unforgiveness in our hearts. It stops the flow of love in and through us. By refusing to forgive, we keep others at bay and block our ability to hear from God.

We should consider this question. *Do I want freedom from hurt and bitterness, or do I prefer the slow deterioration of my spirit, which will render me empty and alone-separated from God and everyone else?* The obvious choice is freedom. We all want freedom from the debilitating effects of bitterness. How can we possibly achieve that which is seemingly impossible? There is a verse I love dearly, which has been my helpful companion when faced with the need to offer acquittal and unable to accomplish it on my own. *"For God is working in you, giving you the desire to obey Him, and the power to do what pleases Him."* Philippians 2:13.

We need God's incredible power to walk the path of forgiveness. Our first step is in *choosing* to forgive the offender. The next step is to ask God for his divine intervention. He will give us the *desire* to forgive much like wrapping a wide, sturdy belt around our will of choice and securing it. Then God's power comes into play eventually dissolving the scars and the wounds over time. One day we wake up and realize we haven't given the offense a thought in weeks or months. The nagging pain reminding us of the wound is gone. The stab of indifference toward the one who injured us has disappeared. Only God has the power through the Holy Spirit to enable us to come to this point of complete acquittal for the offender.

There is no greater gift we can give our spirit than to forgive another person. There is no greater gift we can give our spirit than to forgive *ourselves*. The liberation which comes to the heart is absolutely life changing. We begin the work by a choice of our will, and God will complete it by the power of his healing, changing grace.

(2)

"You must make allowance for each other's faults and forgive the person who offends you. Remember the Lord forgave you, so you must forgive others. And the most important piece of clothing you must wear is love. Love is what binds us together in perfect harmony." Colossians 3: 13-14.

She cuddled up to her blanket, safe and warm in her little bed. The nightlight by the corner dresser illuminated the darkness with soft, comforting warmth. Just as her eyelids were closing, giving in to the peaceful rest of sleep, she heard him coming up the stairs. He was walking softly so not to be heard. Her heart

133

began to beat hard in her small chest and she quickly pushed the covers back in order to make a hasty escape to the safety of the locked bathroom. Before she could put a foot on the cold floor he was there. His hand covered her mouth, silencing her pleas. "Don't cry, Clara. I won't hurt you. Just lay back and be still."

His rough and calloused hands made their way over her tiny frame. His breath was rank with the smell of liquor. Nothing was sacred to him. He climbed on top of her and invaded her little body once again. Without a single word of remorse he sat up, turned and walked back down the stairs. She pulled her pink covers up to her neck and huddled into a protective ball.

Clara should be used to it all by now. He had been coming into her room since she was only five. Her father, a man she loved and adored, died unexpectedly in a tragic car accident. Her mother quickly remarried, unable to financially support the family on her own. At first, Frank was sweet and gentle. He read her stories while he held her in his lap. She loved his deep voice and the way he made the characters in the pictures come alive. The first time, he told her that what he was doing was all right; it was simply his way of expressing his love for her. She should be happy to have someone who loved her so deeply. *I wish he hated me. Maybe then he would leave me alone.*

Months swiftly turned into years and the child became a woman. Clara hoped the abuse would stop, but instead it escalated. Barely a night went by without his intrusion into her life and her body. Her mother didn't believe her stories when she was a small child so she had long ago given up on the protection and security of maternal instincts.

It seemed her only hope of escape was to marry. Her boyfriend, young and inexperienced was completely unaware of her torment. He loved her for the wonderful person she was and quickly agreed to the union. They set the date and proceeded with their plan. She informed her abuser of the upcoming nuptials, thinking this would somehow deter his misplaced affection. However, the night before her wedding Frank stalked into her bedroom, and took her for the last time.

Years went by, her marriage somehow surviving the torment of the past. She became a mother, protective and loving. Realizing she needed healing from the abuse, Clara finally spoke to her husband about the horrible events of her childhood. Understandably, he wanted to kill the man, but she restrained him, having learned a great deal about the ghosts that haunted her stepfather.

Frank's own childhood was riddled with sexual abuse and physical beatings so severe it was incredible he survived. He drank to cover the torment of his suppressed memories and continued the cycle of abuse as it was all he had ever known. Clara didn't excuse his behavior. How could she? But she did learn to forgive it. With the help of a loving counselor, a gift from the hand and heart of God, she began to see the depths of her stepfather's pain. With intense counsel, Clara learned to successfully deal with her own. When she was strong enough, she finally confronted him.

It had been many long years since she stood in the front yard of that little, grey house. Everything appeared smaller somehow. She slowly climbed the withered stairs to the front door, and with a firm hand rang the doorbell. She took a deep breath and opened the door. "Frank, are you here? It's Clara. I need to talk to you."

"Clara, what are you doing here?" he asked, his voice shaky and filled with disbelief. He slowly made his way into the living room. Sara was surprised at the aging man standing before her. Small and grey haired, he was fragile in appearance. She could see the fear in his eyes.

"I need you to know something. I forgive you for what you did to me when I lived in this house. You crossed the line. You did things no one should ever do to a child. It's inexcusable, really, but I've managed to work past it, and I have a family of my own now. No one will ever hurt my little girl like you hurt me. Kind people have helped me to see that I wasn't the only one who suffered. I know you dealt with a lot of pain when you were little, too. Maybe that's the reason you hurt me." Tears were welling up in his eyes as he turned away from Clara.

"You must leave here. Don't ever come back. I'm a sick old man who isn't worth your time or energy. Don't expect an apology because I don't have any to give you. Just live your life, Clara, just live your life." He held up his hand indicating his inability to cope with Clara's sincere acquittal. With staggering gait, he turned and made his way up the stairs to the bedroom. Falling on the bed he waited until he heard the front door shut. Sobs racked his body as he reached for the bottle and deftly silenced the pain.

◆◆

Human frailty is unfortunately part of our journey. Some mistakes are far more serious than others, and no one is completely above reproach. Circumstance and situations beyond our control often play a role in our unworthy decisions. They are not an avenue for excuse, but rather a path in need of examination. God is there in our pain and suffering to forgive the events that haunt our memories. He is able to take us beyond our pain to a place of acquittal for those who have, for whatever reason, abused our hearts, minds and bodies. *"You must make allowance for each other's faults and forgive the person who offends you. Remember the Lord forgave you, so you must forgive others."* Colossians 3: 13.

Love is a life force that operates most purely when accompanied by an acquitting heart. The one hurt most by unforgiveness is the one who is not willing to forgive. If we can somehow make allowances for the weaknesses of others, we can then come to a place of complete release. The burden we carry in our hearts can be replaced with the peaceful rest of pardon.

The act of love coupled with a forgiving heart covers a multitude of hurts, allowing us the freedom to move forward, liberated from the past. As we forgive, God forgives us.

(3)

"The steps of the godly are directed by the Lord. He delights in every detail of their lives. Though they stumble, they will not fall, for the Lord holds them by the hand." Psalms 37:23-24.

One may wonder what the above verse has to do with the topic of forgiveness. Along the journey of life, it's clear to see how God in his omniscient way perfectly plans the course of events to bring us to the point of enlightenment. Since he is well aware of every hidden thing in the concealed parts of our heart, God's spirit is the only true informant of our most intimate nature. Just as the wind blows through the trees caressing every leaf, so the spirit of God moves through the heart of man revealing all that is hidden. In the story below, God used long past acquaintances to reveal some remaining unforgiveness in my heart.

◆◆

Sara and Dan, people we knew many years ago, phoned to let us know they were in town and wanted to come and visit. We had not seen them for a long time and were never close to them when we lived in the same town. Sara and Dan are lovely people, but our relationship was casual at best. Our lives are very full with work, children, and other responsibilities; so an interruption of our time is not something we relish. However, they were persistent so we acquiesced and set up a short visit over coffee and pie.

"How in the world are you?" I asked, genuinely bemused to see them.

"You haven't changed a bit!" Sara chided. "How long has it been since we had a chance to talk?" She asked.

"Oh goodness, I think it's been at least ten years since we last ran into each other. Can you believe how time flies?" I marveled. After a while we began to speak of events and people in the past we had all known. A topic arose which had caused a great deal of distress and tremendous pain at the time it occurred, and I found myself becoming defensive and even angry over things long forgotten. The place of worship we attended had an unpleasant and unexpected upheaval common to men in leadership, yet tremendously hurtful to those who willingly entrust their confidence.

After they left, I sat in the solitude of the back porch for a long time and contemplated my angry reactions to our discussion. Something became very clear to me. It was not by accident that these people had come to visit us. Though I was not aware of areas of unforgiveness in my heart, God was *keenly* knowledgeable of it. He wanted to bring to my attention those things that were troubling me; keeping me from my full potential. God orchestrated that meeting to enlighten me of a dark room still remaining, needful of the exposure of his light and love in order to set me free from the past. *"The steps of the godly are directed by the Lord. He delights in every detail of their lives."* Psalms 37:23.

◆◆

Our God is a God of particulars. He has skillfully crafted us and is fully aware of every event of our lives, and the possible ramifications of those events upon our spirit. Past, present or future does not dictate God's time line. He sees all events simultaneously laid out before him. With this remarkable ability, God can finely tune the course of our lives if we entrust our hearts and subsistence to his safekeeping. His tremendous attention to detail surpasses our limited ability to comprehend his enormous compassion for his creation. God truly does *direct* our path as we walk before him with pure intentions and absolute trust. He takes great pleasure in liberating us from the past and setting our course toward a better direction.

Through the passing of time, the unforgiveness in my heart would eventually impair my ability to love. A root of bitterness toward the offenders and offences of my past had immobilized my spirit, confining me without my knowledge of the root of the problem. *"Though they stumble, they will not fall, for the Lord holds them by the hand."* Verse 24. It is the Lord's hand that pulls us up and leads us to revelatory events, bringing our spirits to a point of complete release. He wants us to be free to live and love and give with open hearts, unencumbered by any weight. It wasn't by accident Sara and Dan came by for a visit that day. God planned it to set my spirit free.

Father I pray you will continue to expose those dark rooms of the heart of my spirit to the light of your love. Lead me by your gentle hand toward a path of freedom as you reveal the obstacles standing in my way. Remove the weights and restraints that prevent me from being all you have designed me to be. Employ your

*brand of forgiveness into my heart concerning anyone or any-
thing I am aware of or unaware of, which still impedes my walk
with you. Let forgiveness begin in me today.*

(4)

*"Never pay back evil for evil to anyone. Do things in such a way
that everyone can see you are honorable. Do your part to live in
peace with everyone, as much as possible. Dear friends, never
avenge yourselves. Leave that to God. For it is written, "I will
take vengeance; I will repay those who deserve it," says the Lord.
Instead, do what the scriptures say, 'If your enemies are hungry
feed them. If they are thirsty, give them something to drink, and
they will be ashamed of what they have done to you.' Don't let
evil get the best of you, but conquer evil by doing good."* Romans
12:17-21.

Jeri was working diligently on her Bachelor's Degree in education. Young and energetic, she was looking forward to a
hands-on experience with students and teaching supervisors. Part
of the obligation was a three-month teaching stint with a local high
school. Jeri's the type of girl who is extremely easy to get along
with, conscientious to a fault and disgustingly prompt. You'd have
to look long and hard to find anything to complain about.

Day one of her venture began on a hopeful note, until Jeri's
supervising instructor stepped forcefully into the room. With a
loud, grating voice she exclaimed, "Well, the first thing you need
to do young lady is to crop that pathetic long hair off and dye it a
human color." Jeri sat in stunned silence as the woman went on to
belittle her wardrobe, her shoes and most everything else visible
about her. *This should be an interesting three months,* Jeri mused.

No matter what her supervisor required, Jeri went above and
beyond the call of duty. When the supervisor requested a month
long calendar of daily teaching assignments, Jeri added extra-cur-
ricular activities for the students as well. Pleased with her effort,
she proudly handed this labor-ridden project to her supervisor.

139

Without missing a beat and with barely a glance, the woman tossed the calendar in the trashcan and declared, "If that's the best you can do, perhaps you'd better find a different profession, young lady!" Day after exhausting day, Jeri tried unsuccessfully to placate this bitter, resentful woman.

She began to have vengeful thoughts about this person. Perhaps a letter to the school board would be in order. A multitude of various scenarios ran through Jeri's mind as she tried to imagine what could possibly have created this monster before her. Did she suffer through a nasty divorce? Were here parents intolerably abusive? However, these questions were far too personal to ask, when barely a *"hello"* emerged from those tight, thin lips. Jeri was left to her own imaginations.

The one ray of hope in this dismal dungeon was the students-bright, eager, funny, and loving. They were her salvation. They appreciated her and made Jeri feel loved and respected.

Day after day she put her best foot forward, and day after day the supervisor stepped on her toes. There was no way to win this battle.

At the welcome end of her tenure she came before the board of the school to discuss her student teaching experience. She made a concerted effort to say something nice about her supervisor, but what could she say? The board sat looking at her quizzically, with a hint of admiration in their eyes. "How did you do it?" they asked. "No one before you has survived her. One student teacher had a nervous break-down; another left in tears on the second day, and the third decided after the first two weeks teaching was not for him."

Jeri sat quietly in her chair and thought for a few reflective moments before replying. "One thing I'm sure of. I would make a heck of a teacher. I love kids, and I have a gift for teaching. No one, not even *that woman,* can take that away from me."

Shortly after Jeri's departure, the school board made the necessary decision to terminate the supervisor's position, suggesting she find a new line of employment.

◆◆

God does not expect us to lie down and become a doormat for anyone. Each of us has been given gifts and talents that deserve respect and consideration. Unfortunately, not everyone chooses to regard our faculties or even acknowledge them. However, if we are cognizant of our own contributions, skills, and abilities, much like Jeri in the above story, we do not have to cower when placed in a position of disrespect. In other words, it is someone else's problem if they don't grasp our worth and value. We can still go forward and be the very best we can be. If we lay hold of this truth, there is nothing that can stand in our way.

We have no need to take vengeance into our own hands, but to walk honorably and upright in a manner pleasing before God. We can be confident in our position before our Creator. By standing tall in the face of adversity, relying fully on God's omniscient abilities, we always have the upper hand. Even if we don't see the answer immediately, we can be assured God is at work to bring about the necessary changes in our hearts and in the lives of those who carelessly harm us.

It takes a great deal of courage, self-control, and integrity to put to practice the last part of the above verse. *"If your enemies are hungry feed them. If they are thirsty, give them something to drink."* By making the choice to carry through with this command, the scripture continues on to say, *"they will be ashamed of what they have done to you."* In other words, God will do *his* part to bring conviction and justice to the heart of our offender, if we are disciplined in walking through with his principles.

Jeri did her job with forthright integrity, and solid constitution. She made no effort to inflict pain or avenge her treatment. Consequently, she was honored with her teaching certificate and went on to accomplish her goals. The supervisor, on the other hand, lost her position due to the poor choices she made. Our greatest weapon in the face of reproach is *prayer* for the offender, layered with *kindness*, *integrity*, and *forgiveness*. If we choose the better path, God will, in his perfect timing, handle the rest.

"Come now let us talk about this (argue this out), says the Lord. No matter how deep the stain of your sins, I can remove it. I can make you as clean as freshly fallen snow. Even if you are stained as red as crimson, I can make you as white as wool." Isaiah 1:18.

Imagine walking in a hot, steamy, dirty desert for many days with no water to wash in and no water to drink. Perspiration covers every inch of your body, and your feet ache from the misery of the march. Your clothing is stiff and rank from the magnitude of grime accumulated during the journey. The only goal, to get a drink of cool, refreshing water, strip those nasty clothes off, and dive into a bath to clean away the filth.

This is the perfect description for the spiritual state of man before God comes in and offers his cleansing forgiveness. God is responsive to pardon us if we are willing to acknowledge our imperfections and failures, and ask for his release. Why is it so difficult for us to admit our shortcomings? Why do we struggle so defiantly over those two little words; *I'm sorry?* Pride jumps out of the depths of our soul and stands aggressively in the way, blocking our path to peace. If we make a willful choice to circumvent pride, simply by speaking up when we are wrong, we free ourselves from the entrapments of this human barrier.

In seeking God's forgiveness and cleansing for our transgressions, we have his full, undivided attention. He simply casts our iniquity into the *sea of forgetfulness*, never to be remembered again. What an awesome thought. God doesn't remind us of our past mistakes if we fail again. He washes us clean, like the shower after the desert trek. He gives us a fresh, crisp, white robe of righteousness, placing us in right-standing with our God. He exchanges our worn-out shoes of contention with beautiful sandals of peace.

Once we've asked for God's forgiveness, it is time to take the next step, self-acquittal. It is often much easier to forgive others than it is to absolve ourselves. The key is the realization that absolution comes from a loving Father who is willing to acquit us, if we are willing to seek acquittal. Let us apply the same principle discussed in segment one of this chapter on forgiveness. *"For God is working in you, giving you the desire to obey Him, and the power to do what pleases Him."* Philippians 2:13.

We first make the plea for forgiveness before God, then we direct our will toward our own offence, requesting his divine intervention to give us the *desire* to forgive ourselves. God walks in at that moment and empowers us to step out of the shell of condemnation and walk away from the past. Speaking from experience, it is challenging to step away from our self-imposed exile and receive this liberating gift.

When my daughter was growing up, I had many interests I wanted to pursue. Everything I had worked so hard for was suddenly put on hold. As everyone knows a child comes first. As much as I loved her, I resented that my husband could go to work everyday, fulfill his destiny and pursue his talents, while I sat at home caring for a toddler.

As soon as I possibly could, I was back at it, pushing and driving toward my goals of success. I made sure she was in good hands, and that I could be with her as much as possible, but the focus was on my pursuits rather than my child.

Now that she's a teen, I look back on all those hours I could have enjoyed her company, making her laugh that sweet baby laugh and playing games with her. There's simply no way to go back and recapture lost moments. I will always regret the immaturity of my decision. However, it was just that, *immaturity*.

Forgiving my heart for the many blunders of the past has been a continual exercise in frustration. I am only *now* learning to apply these scriptures to free my spirit from the bondage of unforgiveness and work through my own pain.

Matthew 6:14-15 states if we are unwilling to forgive, we cannot be forgiven. We need to realize this applies to our own errors as well. God desires absolute, uncompromising freedom for his children. The only way to walk in complete emancipation of the spirit is to *cross the sea of forgiveness.* God supplies the mode of transportation. All we have to do is be willing and obedient to get in the boat.

You gotta lighten the load to walk on the water!

Diving Into Health and Healing

chapter ten

(1)

"A cheerful heart is good medicine, but a broken spirit saps a person's strength." Proverbs 17:22.

Attitude is extraordinarily important when dealing with illness, and it is the continual key to walking in health. Confident trust in God enables us to move forward with a positive and conclusive mental disposition.

I know people who face illness with despair and hopelessness. I have seen them deteriorate rapidly, their broken spirit and wounded heart neglecting the urgency and necessity of faith. They have turned their backs on God, because they believe God has turned his back on them. Not true. God *never* turns his back on his creation. His out-stretched arms offer constant hope of renewal and relationship.

What creates a positive attitude? **Faith.** *"What is faith? It is the confident assurance that what we hope for is going to happen. It is the evidence of things we cannot yet see. God gave his approval to people in days of old because of their faith."* Hebrews 11:1-2.

When we were children, we placed trust in our parents or caretakers to provide for our needs and desires. (I realize not everyone reading this will have had the blessing of that type of paternal relationship, but most people can think of someone they could put their confidence in.) Likewise, God desires childlike reliance that looks to him to provide what we need and even much of what we want. Who doesn't *want* to walk in health? Who doesn't *need* to be healed? Health and healing begin in the spirit of an individual. The best place to start is by looking up into the face of our loving Father who knows our needs before we ask. *"He is touched by the feelings of our infirmities."* Hebrews 4:15a. Below is a quick allegory expressing the weighty effects of illness upon the spirit.

◆◆

Not long ago Janie called her friend Cathee, very distraught and in pain. She had been suffering terribly with agonizing periods due to a large cyst on her ovary. Every two weeks without fail she had another period, and as most women can relate, she was often exhausted and cranky. Newly married, the whole situation was putting undo stress on her relationship, and making it difficult to be a patient and understanding mother to her son from a previous marriage.

Janie had made several visits to the doctor, who suggested these situations would often work themselves out without surgery. He placed her on medication asking her to wait a while in hopes the cyst would dissolve on its own. Meanwhile, her suffering went on for months. She and her new husband desperately wanted a baby of their own and this hope was all but crushed due to her malady. She came over to Cathee's home despairing over her situation, but fully confident God was able to turn her difficulty around.

"I have dealt with this problem for such a long time now. I am simply miserable. My weight is fluctuating, due to the water retention. My little boy doesn't know which mommy he will have from day to day-the nice one or the shrew. I feel terrible when I snap off his head with some impatient remark, and my new husband isn't sure *what* he's gotten himself into."

Cathee and Janie walked out to the lanai and sat on the sofa. Janie's face was worn with exhaustion and her countenance was heartbreaking. They talked awhile about God's ability to turn things around and to restore hope when all hope was gone. "I have certainly seen a lot of miraculous things happen when people pray," said Cathee, and she began to tell Janie some of the stories of supernatural intervention she had been privileged to witness first hand. After a while, Janie asked if they could pray about her current struggle. The women prayed a simple prayer together, asking God for his divine intervention on Janie's behalf. They asked Him to take the cyst away and restore her health. There was nothing fancy about the prayer, no special words or formulas, just two women desperate for an answer from God.

Janie was due to return to the doctor in two days for a follow-up ultrasound. Much to her amazement the cyst was gone, completely gone, with no sign it had ever been present. Her periods normalized immediately and within a few months she was pregnant. Holding her baby girl confirmed God's great love and his ability to both hear and answer prayer. *Nothing is impossible with God.*

By maintaining an attitude of positive faithfulness toward God, by actually *believing* in his ability to heal, we literally pour the good medicine of a cheerful heart into this house of flesh. This faith enables us to trust him to keep us, whether we walk through illness or health. And God *always* rewards our faith in his way, and time.

(2)

"'My gracious favor is all you need. My power works best in your weakness.'" II Corinthians 12:9a.

A few years ago, I worked in a lovely hotel in St. Louis and had the opportunity to become friends with the personnel director and his wife. They were wonderful people and often took time from their busy schedule for some coffee and conversation. One particular evening, he came into work with a long and despondent face. I knew something wasn't right, as he was always a positive, upbeat kind of guy. When I asked what the problem was, he began to unfold a sad and frightening story. His lovely wife,

Laurie, had just been diagnosed with breast cancer, and the prognosis was not good. It had not been detected as early as the doctors would have liked. I could tell by his countenance he was coming to terms with the reality of enormous change in both their lives. He was fearful of what the future might bring.

I was so troubled by his news; I tossed and turned all night. Sleep completely eluded me. I kept seeing her beautiful face and flowing blonde hair, and I *knew* in my heart, God had a plan and purpose for all of this. I was compelled to write her a letter and tell her of a miraculous event, one in which God supernaturally intervened and brought healing to someone in his darkest hour of need. As I related to her, cancer is no big deal to God. I got up out of my bed in the wee hours of the morning and wrote the letter, mailing it as soon as possible.

After only a few days, she called. "I just received the note you sent me, and I must say I am both intrigued and touched. I am so glad you told me the story about the man healed of cancer, and I would really like to know more of the details. Perhaps we could get together and talk about it." I went on to tell her of the others I had seen healed of various diseases over the years. I said I knew God was totally able to restore her health and bring her into a completely new understanding of his love. She agreed to attend a woman's luncheon with a teacher who was seasoned in her knowledge of scripture and the character of God. I had been attending these teachings on a regular basis and there were always ten to twelve women at each meeting. This time there was no one but Laurie, the teacher, and me. What was God up to?

Sometimes when God sets the stage for his divine intervention, situations and circumstances are completely contrary to what we may expect. We think we know just how the story should unfold, but God steps in and everything changes.

After the teacher was finished with a beautiful, uplifting instruction, Laurie began to ask some deep and personal questions about the reality of healing and its relationship to faith. She started to open her heart in intimate ways she would never have, if there had been other women in attendance. She began to share her secret hurts and wounds, laying her life bare before us. Her transparency and honesty opened the door of conversation with God that allowed the miraculous to happen. She chose to *believe* God loved her and desired an in-depth and profoundly personal bond with her. This spiritual connection would directly impact every other aspect of her life. She accepted that love and reached out in her weakness toward His loving hands of strength. The Lord wrapped his arms around her that day, and she began to walk a new path; one filled with hope, joy, peace and *healing*.

That event took place roughly ten years ago. She is walking in health and vitality today, with no further recurrence of cancer. Sometimes the very event we think will destroy us is the thing that brings us to an encounter with the giver of life and the source of our existence. *"My gracious favor is all you need. My power works best in your weakness.'"* II Corinthians 12:9a.

(3)

"He heals the brokenhearted, binding up their wounds." Psalms 147:3.

Broken hearts cause distress to the spirit and can certainly result in illness. Our body suffers greatly for the past and present hurts we carry within our spirits. Sometimes we are unaware of the debilitating affects of our pain until symptoms manifest in our bodies. The frame visible to the outside world is just the shell, not a true representation of who or what we are. We often choose to hide beneath the facade, burying our pain and sorrow, but eventually there has to be an outlet for the hurt. Studies indicate that many of the diseases people face today are a direct result of unforgiveness, bitterness, anger, sorrow, and other unresolved issues. Below is a story defining the importance of allowing God to heal our broken hearts and restore our troubled souls.

◆◆

A few short months ago, Pam was struggling with overwhelming feelings of exhaustion and irritability. Headaches ruled her day and Tylenol PM® carried her through the nights. Her stomach was in constant knots, alternating with stabbing pain, and she suspected she may be suffering from an ulcer, or ulcer-related illness. She knew something was wrong beyond the average stress of a working mother. She had a clear and compelling feeling there was something more she needed to examine within her own heart.

"Everyday it's the same old thing. I can't seem to get with it. My head is aching, and I can't eat much. I guess I need to go see my physician again, but I was just there a couple of months ago, and she couldn't find anything wrong with me. She felt I was suffering from a stress-related problem. Her suggestion was a vacation! Great idea, but who has the time for a holiday when you have two kids to deal with?"

"Maybe you are in need of a vacation, right there in your own home," her friend reasoned. Pam looked incredulous.

"What in the world are you talking about? Who in their right mind can relax in the middle of bedlam?"

Her friend was referring to the need to carve out some quiet, uninterrupted down time. A time when the phone isn't ringing, the laundry buzzer isn't blaring, and children aren't banging on the front door-a time for contemplation, soul searching, and some prayer.

"The only chance I could imagine quiet of that magnitude is in the middle of the night, or the early hours of the morning."

"Precisely," her friend affirmed.

It was clear Pam was thinking about all this as she headed out the door that afternoon.

Right away, she put the plan to work. She got up in the middle of the night, wrapped a blanket around her shivering body, and poured herself a cup of hot cocoa with whipped cream. *What in the world am I doing here? I need to be sleeping.* Instead, she found a quiet corner of the living room, sat in her husband's favorite easy chair, and began a discourse with God. She began to ask him about her headaches, stomach problems, and basic malaise. There was only silence from God that night. No lights shone from heaven. No voice boomed revelation.

The next night, Pam woke again. She wore her flannel paja-
mas to bed this time, so she wouldn't freeze as she tiptoed over
to her husbands chair for another quiet rendezvous with God.
Show me what's going on here, please. I need some insight.
Again, only the gentle hum of the refrigerator filled the air as she
sat waiting for something, *anything* from the God. She picked up
the old *Bible* her grandmother had given her as a child and
opened it to the book of Psalms. This was her favorite book, the
one she could most relate to. Psalms 139 drew her into its comforting embrace.

*"Lord, you have examined my heart and know everything
about me. You know when I sit down or stand up. You know my
every thought when far away. You chart the path ahead of me and
tell me where to stop and rest. Every moment you know where I
am. You know what I am going to say even before I say it, Lord.
You both precede and follow me. You place your hand of blessing
on my head. Such knowledge is too wonderful for me. Too great
for me to know."*

There is such peace in trusting the God of all creation with
such a simple task. *Who better to reveal to me the secrets of my
heart, than the one who knows me best?* Pam thought.

On the third night, she woke up around 2:00 in the morning.
All was quiet. She found her little predictable spot again and sat,
waiting on God. This time, something interesting happened. Like
a movie screen in vivid color, her past began to unfold before her.
People, places and events she had completely forgotten, were
being shown to her in Technicolor®. Though Pam had pushed
aside the memories in her natural mind, her spirit held a bibliog-
raphy of wounds, unforgiveness, anger, and sorrow tightly in its
grip. As the face of each perpetrator came before her, she began
to weep. She wept for the anguish within her spirit, as well as the
grievance held so long against her offenders. Each memory was
accompanied by the need to release the distress to God, and allow
him to work forgiveness in her heart. When the Lord was finally
through and there were no more events, names or faces appear-
ing in Pam's mind, she felt as though she had been in a warm,

cleansing, healing bath of indescribable, liberating change. Not an external cleaning, but a holy, precious and divine intervention of the Spirit of God. When she glanced down at her watch, it was 5:00 in the morning. Three hours had passed, and it felt like fifteen minutes. *Give God a moment of your time and see what wonders he can do with it.*

She called excitedly that morning to tell her friend of the wonderful events that had just taken place in her life. "Girl, you won't believe it. God has really met me in my place of need. He showed me all the barriers holding me back and has helped me to forgive the situations of the past and all the people involved. This is the first day I have gotten up without a headache or a stomachache in months. When I looked in the mirror, I didn't even recognize myself. The anger and frustration is simply gone. I feel like a new woman."

God used Pam's physical distress to bring her to a place of seeking his face. That's often how it works. When we finally get tired of being ill, spiritually and physically, and we reach out with hearts of hunger and trust, then our God steps in. He wants us whole, well, happy, peaceful, and full of the beauty of his light and love. He sees the dark corners, tucked away. He is aware of all that we have forgotten. He is able to restore the broken pieces of our wounded spirits. *He heals the brokenhearted, binding up their wounds.* Psalms 147:3.

Take some time and wait on the direction of God. He is faithful to reveal the secrets that debilitate the spirit and impact the body. In order to live in health and healing, it helps to understand that true wholeness is initiated within the heart and is a process begun and completed *by* the Spirit, within the spirit.

(4)

"Praise the Lord, I tell myself; with my whole heart I will praise his holy name. Praise the Lord, I tell myself, and never forget the good things he does for me. He forgives all my sins and heals all my diseases. He ransoms me from death and surrounds me with love and

tender mercies. He fills my life with good things. My youth is renewed like the eagle's." Psalms 103:1-5.

The room was small, the floor dusty, and the walls were covered with dried clay and mud. People were pressed in so tightly; no one could move an elbow. Others outside the door were pushing to get in, afraid they might miss something. Everyone was talking excitedly in anticipation of what they could see and hear. "I heard he raised a little girl from the dead!" "I heard he healed a group of men from leprosy!" *How does he do these things?*

It wasn't long before they got their answers and saw for themselves the power behind the man. Quietly, Jesus stood up and looked over the crowd of thirsty souls. He stepped toward them and began to teach. His eyes were filled with love, and his words rang with a truth and wisdom uncommon to men.

Everyone was trance-like in focused attention. No one could look away from this teacher, so unlike anyone they had heard or seen before.

In the middle of the sermon, debris began to fall on Jesus and the others tightly pressed in the little clay hut. As everyone looked up to see what could be causing the disturbance, a man began to be lowered down through the roof. *Who could be so desperate to do this?* The people quickly glanced back at Jesus to see if he might be upset by this intrusion. Jesus face was filled with a look of both bemusement and admiration.

Seeing the faith of these men, he firmly spoke. *"My son, your sins are forgiven."* Jesus was never one to dwell on the obvious. He looked past the exterior and checked out the condition of the heart, because he understood the state of the body is dictated to by the health of the spirit.

There were those in the crowd whose religious ideals firmly conflicted with Jesus bold statement. They felt he was in over his head by offering to forgive sins. "Who does he think he is? He has no right to make such a statement." But Jesus looked past their righteous robes and calmly explained, *"Is it easier to say to*

153

the paralyzed man, 'Your sins are forgiven' or 'Get up, pick up your mat and walk?"

I think he was trying to get them to see two important things. First, he had the authority to heal and forgive because God had *given* him that authority. Second, Jesus wanted them, and all of us who read about this story, to see how physical illness can be symptomatic of sin.

The paralyzed man looked up into this face of warmth and complete benevolence. These eyes were not like any he had glimpsed before. They saw through the pain and pride. They saw past, present and future all at one time. They understood the suffering and bitterness he had lived with for so long. And, they forgave all.

The man accepted forgiveness, jumped up and grabbed his mat and pushed his way through the astonished crowd. People stood with mouths agape, watching in complete silence as he moved quickly through them. *How can this be?* And yet, they all knew they had been witness to something amazing.

Did the paralyzed man get his healing? Of course he did. But, Jesus healed him from the inside out. He healed the heart of the man, not just the symptoms of his illness. The double result of his healing produced a man who could walk upright physically, and spiritually as well. He reached out in faith and got a lot more than he bargained for.

When we choose a path contrary to God's best for our lives, our spirit is grieved. Eventually, the flesh suffers for our conscious decision to choose disobedience. This is why Jesus said to the paralyzed man, *"your sins are forgiven."* To him, true healing is an act directed toward the spirit, with consequential results that benefit the body.

In seeking forgiveness, we come into a right relationship with God. Our transgression is then taken from us and remembered no more by the heart of God. We are dealt a clean slate and move forward with his love and bountiful blessing. *"Praise the Lord, I tell myself; with my whole heart I will praise his holy name. He forgives all my sins and heals all my diseases. He ransoms me*

*from death and surrounds me with love and tender mercies. He
fills my life with good things."* Psalms 103:10-5.

◆◆

*Father, I pray you will forgive us this day for the transgressions in
our lives from those things we have done to wound your heart and
the hearts of those around us. Heal us from the inside out, and let us
reach forward in faith and receive all that you have purchased for
us through your Son. Begin your work within us today as we submit
our hearts and lives to the hand of a loving and caring Father.*

(5)

*But He was wounded and crushed for our sins. He was beaten
that we might have peace. He was whipped, and we were healed!*
Isaiah 53:5.

His name was Virgil. He was young and handsome, completely full of life and mischief. Everyone knew him as the guy
who was quick with a joke, and always the first one to laugh. He
approached his obligations with conscientious integrity. He was a
guy you could always count on to go the extra mile. His wife
loved him and his boys revered him.

He worked in a plant building bombs for use in World War II.
His job was an important one, and he was proud to help his country, extremely proud.

After a long stint of production, he began to feel a bit tired
and thought perhaps it was the extended hours and difficult labor.
After a few months and noticeable weight loss, Virgil and his
wife thought it best he saw a doctor in the area.

The doc, though well trained in the usual malaise, couldn't
come up with a solution to Virgil's ill health. So, he was sent to
the big city for further analysis. After some intense testing, the
conclusion was ominous, leukemia, cancer of the blood caused
by TNT toxic poisoning. Interestingly, the other two men at his
job were diagnosed with the same disease and within a few
short months, passed away.

In those days leukemia was a death sentence, because medicine was not advanced to the stages of bone marrow transplants, and other sorts of marvelous technology. Seeing his buddies die before him was a frightening experience. On those dark and troublesome days, when faith was elusive, Virgil wondered if he might meet the same fate.

The doctors quickly admitted him to the hospital for intense treatment. And, for six months he lingered there, far from his hometown, receiving numerous blood transfusions and various medicines under the watchful care of his nurses and attending physicians.

This beautiful man with the dark wavy hair and the six foot, three-inch frame now resembled a frail, ailing fellow, a mere shell of the person he once was. He had lost nearly sixty pounds and was a disarming color of orange. Many prayers had been said over him, and he truly had a desire to live, but in all of this, his physicians gave him the unfavorable report. *You must go home and prepare yourself and your family for your impending death. There's nothing more we can do for you. You have only a few more weeks to live.*

Frightened and weary, he traveled back home to ready himself for the inevitable. However, somewhere in the tempest, an encouraging ray of hope illuminated the darkness. He knew God was powerful and able to heal. He had been witness to miracles. He knew many prayers had been offered up for his recovery, and Virgil *believed* God had more for his life than this. His wife needed him. His boys needed him.

He asked his wife to take him to their place of worship. He had been there many times before he became ill and missed the gathering of people of faith. He stepped anonymously into the meeting and took his seat. If it weren't for Virgil's wife, most of the people there would not have recognized him. A guest minister was speaking that evening, a young man with faith to fill an October sky and the heart of a young lion. He preached with fervor about the faithfulness of God, and finished his sermon with a determined plea for those who needed a touch from the Master's hand. Virgil painfully made his way to the front of the building. He requested prayer for his obvious disease. The young minister could not hide his shock at the man's frightening appearance. Obligingly, he prayed, placing his hands on Virgil's fevered brow.

"Father, you see your servant before you. He is in need of a touch from your hand. He has come here in faith, because he knows you are able to turn this situation around and make him whole again. I ask you, Jesus, to take this disease from him and give him back the life he once had."

As Virgil stood before God and the minister, an odd thing took place. The feeling of hot oil began to flow down his body, from the top of his head all the way to the bottom of his feet, causing his toes to actually tingle. He stood perfectly still, in awe of the sensation. When the prayer was over and the presence was gone, he went back to his seat. His step was a little lighter and his countenance was hopeful. He looked at his wife and made a declaration of faith. *I believe God has healed me.*

Naturally, the wife was surprised, and decidedly optimistic. *Did something really happen?* Immediately the next day, Virgil woke without the compelling nausea so prevalent in every moment before this one. He had a ravenous appetite; something he had not had for many months. Each day, he was able to ingest more and more food, and felt better and better. His strength was returning with excited momentum and within a few short months he had regained all the weight he had lost. His color was excellent, his hair had grown back, and there was no visible sign of illness.

He decided a trip to the doctor's office was in order. After the long drive, he walked with a sure foot up the stairs, bounding two at a time, pleased with his own strength. He flung open the door with an assertive gesture and greeted the nurse receptionist with a broad smile. She was on the phone at the time and stopped in mid-sentence, dead silent, as she gazed with shock at the man standing before her.

"Virgil? Virgil Hampton? It can't possibly be you. You have to be dead. Oh, my dear God." She jumped from her seat and ran into the other room, pulling the Doctor from his patient and pushing him into the waiting room. The Doctor stood staring at Virgil with utter amazement. He didn't speak for a long time, just stood gazing intently at the vision before him, studying him from head to toe.

"Well, Virgil, I don't know what possibly could have happened to you, but let me say this. You are a walking miracle. I've seen a few in my life, but never as dramatic as this."

Naturally, the doctor wanted to run elaborate tests on him and try to discover the source of his miraculous recovery. Virgil said, "No, I've got to get back to my family and get on with this gift I've been given."

He returned home to raise his two sons and live a full and productive life.

Virgil was my father. At the time of these events, I was not even born. My oldest brother was six, and my other brother was one year. I have been entrusted with a legacy of faith. This book would never be written if my father had not had the tenacity to hold the hand of God in absolute trust, according to the promises that are written in the scripture. *But he was wounded and crushed for our sins. He was beaten that we might have peace. He was whipped, and we are healed!* Isaiah 53:5.

Because dad took the dive of faith into health and healing, he is still kicking at the resplendent age of 85.

Footloose and fancy-free!

Journey to a Right Relationship with God

chapter eleven

(1)

"Those who obey the law will be declared right in God's sight. Even when Gentiles, who do not have God's written law, instinctively follow what the law says, they show that in their hearts they know right from wrong. They demonstrate that God's law is written within them for their own consciences either to accuse them or tell them they are doing what is right. The day will surely come when God, by Jesus Christ will judge everyone's secret life." Romans 2:13b-16a.

The wind was howling with ferocious velocity as he stood facing the storm. Debris was flying around him, threatening his safety with each pass. There was no relief in site. The only protection available was a tightly woven, over-sized black umbrella with heavy metal handle and veins. He stood as close to the building as possible hoping for some relief, but the wind was merciless, and he was without human aid or concern. He stood alone facing the elements, grateful for the guardianship of his black umbrella.

As the storm continued, the man saw what appeared to be a tiny ray of light shooting its welcome arrow into the bleak darkness. It beckoned him with the promise of a new day. Disregarding the quiet voice compelling him to stand firm, he carefully lowered the umbrella, his only source of protection. With head bowed, he swiftly made his way toward the light. The wind saw its opportunity and grasped the umbrella in its powerful grip, tossing his black guardian over the side of the building, just out of his tortured grasp. He stood, soaked and defeated, his only protection gone and the laughter of the wind tormenting his troubled spirit.

◆◆

We're heading for difficulty when we willingly choose to tune out the warnings of our hearts, venturing in directions contrary to the conscience. During times of such disregard, we move away from God's heart and his best for our lives, much like the man with the umbrella. Symbolically, God is our umbrella, offering his divine protection over our lives. He is impervious to the wind and rain of our troubled existence. There is no bending or shifting with him, regardless of circumstance.

The conscience of man is in direct communication with the heart of God. And in this path of discourse, God's deepest longing for his children is revealed. As the opening scripture explains, the finger of God literally carves his wishes and his laws on the spiritual heart of each individual before a single breath is taken. *They demonstrate that God's law is written within them, for their own consciences either accuse them or tell them they are doing what is right.* Romans 2:15 We *know* what we should and shouldn't do as surely as creation is aware of the power and majesty of its Creator.

Who in their right mind would step out from under this protection in the midst of a raging storm? No one. And yet, every time we choose a direction we sense is contrary to the leading of our heart, this is exactly what we are doing. Like the man in the opening story of this segment, we are stepping out from under God's protective umbrella instead of listening to the wise whisper urging us in the right direction. We are subjecting ourselves to the consequences of our deliberate actions.

Obedience is connected to God's blessing and the closeness of his embrace. Disobedience takes us from that position of safety, leaving us to our own recognizance. Does God walk away? No. He continues to woo us back to the safety of his umbrella and the comfort of his arms. The further we stray, and the longer we stay away, the easier it is to forget how it felt to be protected and loved-to shut out the voice of our conscience.

Our first goal then, in order to walk in a right relationship with God, should be to tune our conscience into the voice of God and listen for his directives. Once we hear those directives, we need to be completely obedient to his leading. The more we obey, the easier we are led by His spirit.

We have a great source as to the heart of God. Scripture-found in the sacred writings of the *Bible*-has the ability to equip and establish us in our quest for walking in tune with the voice of our Creator. If we take time to meditate on the good word of the Lord and ask for his direction in all we do, we are able to set our course toward a right relationship with a loving God. *"My dear children, I am writing this to you so that you will not sin. But if you do sin, there is someone to plead for you before the Father. He is Jesus Christ, the one who pleases God completely. He is the sacrifice for our sins. He takes away not only our sins but the sins of all the world. And how can we be sure that we belong to him? By obeying his commandments. If someone says, 'I belong to God,' but doesn't obey God's commandments, that person is a liar and does not live in the truth. But those who obey God's word really do love him. That is the way to know whether or not we live in him. Those who say they live in God should live their lives as Christ did."* 1 John 2:1-6.

(2)

Why are you trying to find out the future by consulting mediums and psychics? Do not listen to their whisperings and mutterings. Can the living find out the future from the dead? Why not ask your God? Isaiah 8:19.

The sky was pitch black and the only light was the small stars that twinkled in the night as Saul made his clandestine approach to her door. He tapped lightly on the doorpost and waited, tense and edgy, until the door cracked the smallest inch. "What is it you want at this hour of the night?" her voice irritated and fearful.

"I need your help, and I've heard you can predict the future. Let me in, please."

"I don't know who you are and there is a law against such practices. Go away and come back in the daylight." The door shut with a dismissive gesture. However, Saul would not be so lightly discharged.

"Open this door, in the name of the King."

Slowly the door parted, and the woman's face was filled with the fear of recognition. *What are you doing here?* She mentally questioned as she stood, paralyzed with fright.

"There is no one available to tell me the future. My prophet is dead, and God has stopped speaking to me. You are all that's left. You must conjure up Samuel and have him tell me what lies in store for my house and my kingdom."

Reluctantly, she began her incantations and to her great surprise, the prophet Samuel began to materialize. The King and the enchantress trembled before this fearful vision. Without hesitation, Samuel informed Saul of his impending death and the end of his reign. "Tomorrow you will die by your own sword, and your kingdom will be turned over to another. Your two sons will meet their death before the sun sets upon that day."

◆◆

There are so many people seeking the road to enlightenment-the path to God. New Age philosophies abound. Crystals, amulets, incantations, psychic networks, numerology, horoscopes, spiritual gurus, and endless religious philosophies crowd bookstores, radio and television waves, and the internet. Each vehicle promises to have the answer for an assortment of spiritual maladies.

The term "spirituality" is tossed around like the latest Frisbee®, and everyone seems to know exactly what they're talking about. Have there ever been such diverse methodologies available for reaching some form of peace? Each medium holds a measure of merit, and all offer a source of temporary fulfillment and short-term satisfaction. However, if it were possible to have a direct channel to God with the promise of enduring serenity, wouldn't everyone desire to grasp hold of that?

The man in the story was a King named Saul, written about in the first book of Samuel, chapter 28 of the Old Testament *Bible*. Saul was handpicked and appointed by God to be Israel's first King. He did an acceptable job for a while, but soon began to think he was more capable than God and could make better decisions. Repeatedly, he asked God for direction, and immediately set about to make his own subtle changes to God's direct commands.

The prophet Samuel was a holy man, intimate to God's heart and obedient in all things to speak the words of the Lord. Samuel was sent to King Saul to give him this warning: "If your behavior does not begin to line up with God's edicts, you will lose your throne and your kingdom." However, Saul continued his self-righteous behavior, doing exactly what was right in his *own* eyes.

God ceased from all inclinations toward this rebellious King, and in Saul's anger and desperation, he sought the help of a *soothsayer*-someone we would today call a fortuneteller or a psychic. The prophet Samuel had passed away, and Saul felt he had nowhere else to go for revelations about future events. God had spoken specifically to Saul and the constituents of his kingdom *never* to seek the help of mediums, fortunetellers and psychics, because this was a deliberate act of rebellion. Seeking wisdom apart from God demonstrates doubt and unbelief regarding his unlimited power to guide and sustain. In keeping with Saul's pattern of rebellion, he went ahead and sought out the soothsayer.

There are certainly people who possess gifts in spiritual realms. There are those who can predict the future. There are numerous supernatural events and objects of spiritualism available within and beyond our culture. The key to enlightenment is the ability to decipher between *spiritualism* and *spirituality*.

Genuine spirituality has God at the core and faith as its vehicle. Spiritualism is a counterfeit-a mimic of the real thing. It is a decoy and imitation of the perfect, flawless plan of God, and will actually impede our quest for spiritual enlightenment. Spirituality says, *"I see your plan, God. I see your purpose. I understand your power and authority in the earth, and I ask you to guide and direct my life on a daily basis. I will, by faith, joyfully receive your loving protection."* Spiritualism says, *"God, I'll figure out my own plan and design, through my own resources. There are many opportunities for enlightenment, and I will choose the path I find most desirable."*

God provided a way for us to have an authentic relationship with him, through Jesus the Christ. *"Jesus said, 'I am the way, the truth, and the life. No one can come to the Father except through me.'"* John 14:6.

God's desire is for all people to walk by faith, placing their absolute trust in his benevolence and ability to direct their lives on a daily, weekly, monthly and yearly basis. His greatest wish is to be in close communion with his creation, and he has authored the perfect plan to accomplish this goal, accessible and available to all.

(3)

"As the scriptures tell us, 'anyone who believes in him will not be disappointed.' Jew and Gentile are the same in this respect. They all have the same Lord, who generously gives his riches to all who ask for them. For 'Anyone who calls on the name of the Lord will be saved.'" Romans 10:11-13.

Salvation is a term most of us have heard from time to time in our lives, whether or not we are attendees of worship gatherings. The term is strongly associated with Protestant religion, but the fingers of redemption stretch out to every person in each walk of life. Salvation transcends religious barriers and denominational codes. It is no respecter of persons, race, belief, or culture.

God's perfect plan involved sacrifice. He willingly offered up his most treasured possession in order to redeem us, and buy us back from the slavery of transgression. A sacrifice was required to pay the price for our sin. That treasured possession was his only son, born of a woman in order to grasp our human weakness, and allowed to walk in the shoes of humanity to comprehend our struggle. He laid down his pure and faultless life, because a flawless sacrifice was required. *"For God so loved the world that he gave his only Son, so that everyone who believes in him will not perish but have eternal life."* John 3:16.

A mother's love for her children is an all consuming passion, therefore the offering of ones child is incomprehensible to me. The surrender of such love for the ransom of people who have lost their way, is more than I can grasp. However, we are his children also, near and dear to the heart of the Father. He gave One for many. Now the many can be reconciled to God through the One.

This is a promise to *all* persons of *all* creeds, nationalities and beliefs, who are simply willing to be redeemed from iniquity and its strong-hold through faith in the gift Jesus offered to us through his life, death, burial and resurrection. *"For all have sinned: all fall short of God's glorious standard. Yet now God in his gracious kindness declares us not guilty. He has done this through Christ Jesus, who has freed us by taking away our sins. For God sent Jesus to take the punishment for our sins and to satisfy God's anger against us. We are made right with God when we believe that Jesus shed his blood, sacrificing his life for us."* Romans 3:23-25.

And how do we receive this gift? It is as simple as faith itself. God made the path to a right relationship with him a straight and simple one, easy enough for a child to follow. *"For if you confess with your mouth that Jesus is Lord and believe in your heart that God raised him from the dead, you will be saved. For it is by believing in your heart that you are made right with God, and it is by confessing with your mouth that you are saved. As the scriptures tell us, 'Anyone who believes in him will not be disappointed.' Jew and non-Jew alike are the same in this respect. They all have the same Lord, who generously gives his riches to all who ask for them. For 'Anyone who calls on the name of the Lord will be saved.' "* Romans 10:9-13.

So many times we feel we must *earn* a gift. If we do enough good deeds, we can work our way into heaven. This is not true. God has offered this gift freely to us, and there is nothing but faith itself we can trade for our redemption. Does this mean we don't need to concern ourselves with good deeds, kind actions, and words? Of course not. However, good deeds alone won't win us a place in heaven. Salvation is purchased by faith. *"God saved you by his special favor when you believed. And you can't take credit for this: it is a gift from God. Salvation is not a reward for the good things we have done, so none of us can boast about it. For we are God's masterpiece. He has created us anew in Christ Jesus, so that we can do the good things he planned for us long ago."* Ephesians 2:8-10.

What a blessed relief-what a burden that's lifted from our shoulders. We can't *earn* a right relationship with God. We must ask and believe for it, and then walk out the course of day-to-day living with his blessing and guidance. Putting our best foot forward each day in order to please our heavenly Father displays our love for him; and his reciprocal gift is immeasurable, unconditional love toward us.

God's plan is simple, but his benevolence to those who believe is complexingly great. Freedom from the weight of sin is beyond comprehension. To share in God's riches, and the beauty of Heaven as well, surpasses all human reason. We have these promises given freely to us, simply by an act of *faith.*

(4)

"And I am convinced that nothing can ever separate us from his love. Death can't, and life can't. The angels can't and the demons can't. Our fears for today, our worries about tomorrow, and even the powers of hell can't keep God's love away. Whether we are high above the sky or in the deepest ocean, nothing in all creation will ever be able to separate us from the love of God that is revealed in Christ Jesus our Lord." Romans 8:38-39.

He huddled in the thick underbrush of the jungle as the bullets whizzed by his head, hot and menacing. The enemy had them pinned down and there was no way out. This was supposed to be a simple retrieval, but the helicopter carrying the rescue team had been hit by enemy mortar and taken a plunge into the heart of hell. *How did I get here?* Richard wondered. His buddy was bleeding badly. He had stepped on a hidden mine when running from the downed copter and very little was left of his right leg. Richard was putting as much pressure on the wound as possible, but the bleeding simply wouldn't stop.

"Hang in there Steve, we'll make it man."

"We've got a rat's chance of pulling out of this, and you know it." Steve's breathing was labored and his eyes were getting glassy. He was going in and out of consciousness, the life draining from his body.

"Just think about your kids and how much they love you."

"That's all I'm thinking about, man. You'll tell them how much I love them, won't you?" Steve's eyes met Richard's with knowing clarity.

Richard could see his friend was not going to make it, so he said the Lord's Prayer with him, and made the necessary promises to give messages to his loved ones as Steve slipped into that quiet sleep where the body never wakens.

Tears streaming down his face, he held Steve's head to his chest, unwilling to leave, even though his commanding officer was screaming into the walkie-talkie above the sound of the explosions. "Lieutenant, the chopper is here in two. Prepare to depart location and head to pick-up zone." Richard couldn't answer him. How could he leave his friend here in this place of death and destruction?

A quiet and unexpected peace settled over Richard as he took a last look at Steve's untroubled countenance. *You'll never be hurt again, buddy. You're all right now.* On hands and knees, he crawled to join his team, bullets still whizzing precariously close. Somehow they had to make their way to the waiting chopper, the rescuers now the rescued.

♦♦

It was great day for a short trip. The weather was perfect, a typically warm day in the Florida summer. Although the flight forecast registered a possible storm, Jerry would be in Atlanta long before any problems could occur. He took the little Cessna up from the runway with ease and quickly climbed to 4500 feet. This was his favorite escape. No one could touch him here. He was safe from the pressures of work and the cruelties of human opinions. God alone was his worthy co-pilot, and the two of them enjoyed flying.

Just as he reached the tip of Florida, the panhandle clearly in sight, a weather warning came over his radio. "Cessna 182 November, please radio tower. Call flight watch for new route."

"Roger that. This is Cessna 182 November, please vector to nearest airport for possible landing." Jerry had been in situations like this before without incident. He quickly radioed flight watch for a weather update. A class three storm not uncommon this time of year, had whipped up unexpectedly and was moving extremely fast, directly into his flight path.

Out of his right window, a dark menacing cloud was closing in. He hadn't seen it before, though his visibility was excellent. His plane, although an outstanding machine, wasn't a particularly quick bullet. Jerry began to wonder if he could outrun this one.

The plane began to pitch hard to the left, and he made the necessary rudder adjustments. He gave thought to doing a 180-degree turnaround and head back home, but the storm was coming in too fast behind him. There was no way to outrun this girl. She was a dangerous force. All he could do was sit tight and keep control of the plane.

Concentrating intensely on level flight, Jerry couldn't help but remember the tranquility of his previous trips. He was wishing this one was the same. "It's you and me, Lord. We've got a monster on our tail, and no way to get away from her. Stay with me and see me through, whatever happens."

A feeling much like an elevator's rapid assent in a mega high-rise stole over the plane. Jerry was pushed down hard into his seat. He felt the hair on his head stand up, and he involuntarily gasped a deep breath. Looking out the left window, he could see the judgment of the storm. She had catapulted him straight up to the heavens.

"This is Cessna 182 November, I've been caught in an updraft and I'm now at 18,000 feet. My wings are gone. The storm has carried me to the top of the world. God and I are going home. I send my love to my family. Cessna out."

◆◆

It's beautiful to know we never have to face life's challenges alone. No matter what the path may bring, whether we find ourselves in hell's grasp or heaven's view, we always have that comfort of God's presence and love to sustain us. *Whether we are high above the sky or in the deepest ocean, nothing in all creation will ever be able to separate us from the love of God that is revealed in Christ Jesus our Lord.* Romans 8:39. Nothing can tear us out of his embrace, or break the bonds of his ardor. No matter what we may face, or where the journey may take us, God will always be there, our constant companion. Though we may doubt our own fragile ability to face the trials life unavoidably brings, God sees through our weaknesses and endows us with great strength and confident peace.

This is the intimate God we have the good fortune of knowing. He is *genuinely* touched by our pain and suffering, and he legitimately cares about our struggles. *"The Lord is close to the brokenhearted; he rescues those who are crushed in spirit."* Psalms 34:18.

No closer friend and confidant could we ever hope to have. I've been blessed to know dear people over the years that have been available to help me pick up the pieces of my tattered and torn life. However, I have never had a friend like Jesus. In my darkest hours of the night, he has always been there. Through every tear and trauma, he has always been there. When my heart fails me for all the mistakes I make, he never condemns me. Instead, he reaches out a hand of forgiveness and a heart of compassion toward my wounded and dying spirit. He renews me, and lets me drink from the promises of his word until I can stand again. *"The steps of the godly are directed by the Lord. He delights in every detail of their lives. Though they stumble, they will not fall, for the Lord holds them by the hand."* Psalms 37:23-24.

Walking in a right relationship with God is completely attainable. We need to have faith in the gift of salvation purchased for us by the life, death and resurrection of Jesus our Lord. Taking time to read the word of God helps us to gain understanding of his promises. Time alone with God in prayer enables us to plug our spirit into his divine power source, strengthening our hearts for the journey.

King David of the book of Psalms in the Old Testament *Bible* understood the closeness God desires with his people when he wrote these words. *"I will praise you, my God and King, and bless your name forever and ever. I will bless you every day, and I will praise you forever. I will meditate on your majestic, glorious splendor and your wonderful miracles. The Lord is kind and merciful, slow to get angry, full of unfailing love. The Lord is good to everyone. He showers compassion on all his creation. They will tell about your mighty deeds and about the majesty and glory of your reign. The Lord is faithful in all he says; he is gracious in all he does. The Lord helps the fallen and lifts up those bent beneath their loads. The Lord is close to all who call on him, yes, to all who call on him sincerely. He fulfills the desires of those who fear him; he hears their cries for help and rescues them. The Lord protects all those who love him. I will praise the Lord and everyone on earth will bless his holy name forever and forever."* Excerpts from Psalms 145.

There's no place like home!

Bibliography

Touch Point Bible, New Living Translation. Tyndale House Publishers, 1996

The Amplified Bible. Zondervan Publishing, latest print update, 1987

Strongs Exhaustive Concordance of the Bible. James Strong S.T.D., L.L.D. James Abingdon Publishers, Nashville, TN. 1980.1976

Logos Bible Reference Series. Logos Research Systems, Inc. 1998

Lance Armstrong, It's Not About the Bike, My Journey Back to Life. Lance Armstrong with Sally Jenkins. G.P. Putnam's Sons, Copyright 2000. Summary story permission of Penguin Putnam Publishing.

If you enjoyed

Shoes For the Spirit,
Encouragements

pick up another copy for a friend at

BarnesandNoble.com,

Barnes and Noble Stores,
or
Amazon.com